CHAPTER and METAVERSE

CHAPTER and METAVERSE

Legal Trends and Developments
In Web3 and NFTs
2023

David B. Hoppe

FOREWORD

Whether you believe they represent the future of gaming, an alternative investment, new ways of displaying art or a speculative tulip-bulb mania destined to crash and burn, everyone can agree that non-fungible tokens (NFTs) have had an enormous impact. Barely a blip on the radar before 2021, NFTs today continue to expand their reach, and many predict that NFTs will become part of daily life before long.

As I write this, tradeable NFTs, along with the cryptocurrency market and the world economy, have given back many of the value gains they achieved in the post-COVID recovery. Headlines warn that high-value NFTs used as Ethereum loan collateral are in danger of being forcibly sold by peer-to-peer lending platforms to cover precipitous drops in their floor prices. During this same period, however, we're seeing some NFTs from profile picture projects continue to sell for over $1 million.

Will NFTs, as Bill Gates predicts, collapse because they fail to deliver any tangible improvement to the world we live in? Or, as others assert, will digitization and the virtualization of human endeavor elevate NFTs to the status of must-have assets? It is likely the truth lies somewhere in between.

As the regulatory environment coalesces and the business community develops more mature use cases, I expect the market to stabilize, investment opportunities to reemerge, and NFT creation and ownership to continue their march into the mainstream.

This book chronicles the NFT evolution – both a chronological progression and a snapshot of the state of the industry as of late 2022. The chapters here explore how various businesses and industries have leveraged NFTs, where they have succeeded and where they have failed. The book delves beyond events within the NFT realm to consider the issues, challenges, and market dynamics that have contributed to these trends. Author David B. Hoppe, a Web3 lawyer based in San Francisco, draws on his experience supporting clients in NFTs and other cutting-edge media/tech business sectors to provide an entertaining yet informative take on business and legal issues in the space.

Though loosely categorized in three sections, the topics tackled by the author are as diverse as the industry itself. These include both explanations of how pending and resolved legal cases will shape the NFT landscape and eclectic subjects such as the use of NFTs in marketing campaigns and crowdfunding of albums, films, and business startups.

Naoko Okumoto
Board Member, Coindesk Japan
Palo Alto, January 2023

PREFACE

For a phenomenon that has swept the world, brought new creative possibilities for artists and investors, and inspired never-before-seen use cases and business models, it is surprising how little is widely understood about NFTs.

What exactly are NFTs?

A British court said they should be recognized as property. Advocates evangelize that they are the future of property and much human interaction, while cynics relegate them to has-been status. To an outspoken community of old-school gamers, NFTs are yet another manifestation of industry greed. The United States seems to be on a course toward categorizing at least some NFTs as securities.

One thing's for certain—NFTs have become a political, regulatory, and legal football used in a game in which the rulebook remains largely unwritten, and you can't always tell the players even with a scorecard.

While the future of NFTs may be difficult to predict, certain trends, regulatory actions, and court decisions over the last two years provide indications on how developing legal standards are likely to impact the adoption of NFTs and the extent to which they will be allowed to realize their full potential to positively impact our lives.

While many of the essays in this book involve legal issues, I have endeavored to present these discussions in the context of popular culture topics and personalities, like used sneakers, Jay-Z, Quentin Tarantino, Serena Williams, Bill Gates, Justin Bieber, and Nike.

Whether you're interested in intellectual property law, are considering creating or purchasing NFTs, or are just interested in an entertaining perspective on NFTs, I hope you will enjoy this collection of short essays.

David B. Hoppe
San Francisco, April 2023

CONTENTS

MINTERS, INVESTORS, AND GAMERS

Technavio predicts the global NFT market will surpass $110 billion by 2027, fueled by a robust 35 percent CAGR. Even after the market slump in 2022, the research firm says demand for NFT art—spurred by social media— is largely responsible for its rosy outlook. Still, Technavio cautions that "uncertainty in NFT demand and pricing is challenging the market growth. Hence, it is extremely difficult to anticipate the identity of the next buyers of an NFT or the possible factors that can drive their purchase." Indeed, the recovery seemed to reach exit velocity early in 2023, highlighted by the launch of NFT collections from Yuga Labs, Doodles, and other major players.

Who Creates NFTs, and Why?

The *New York Times* archives are filled with thousands of stories in print storage and digital databases. Subscribers can access and read these stories whenever they like. However, on March 24th, 2021, a collector paid more than $500,000 for a non-fungible token (NFT) of the first article the Gray Lady ever published about NFTs and cryptocurrency. The NFT, like other such tokens, grants the owner exclusive digital owner-ship—in this case to a relatively short newspaper

column that remains publicly available. The NFT owner has no claim on the article's copyright or even a physical clipping of the piece. The value, of course, comes from the subject matter and the article's collectability. The astronomical price tag highlights the growing popularity of NFTs. NFT creators—or "minters" as they are known—turn widely consumable digital assets like videos, GIFs, tweets, music, art, and video game features into one-of-a-kind collectible digital items, but who are these minters and what do they get out of it?

What Are NFTs?

An NFT is a unique unit of data that represents a real-world object or item of digital content. NFT developers are revolutionizing how the concept of ownership can be monetized and appreciated. These NFT creators are a unique group with different motivations and goals, but they all are ushering in a new era for the understanding and provable tracking of ownership.

Non-fungible tokens can take something that is mass-produced or mass-consumed and turn it into a unique, rare artifact often by using blockchain technology. Each NFT is built using a custom digital code that is stored on a blockchain such as Ethereum, ensuring it cannot be counterfeited or reproduced. NFTs are neither currencies nor securities in that they can't be exchanged directly for other NFTs. This is what makes them non-fungible. Like an original piece of art or other types of collectibles, their value is primarily in the eye of the beholder and is only worth what someone else is willing to pay for it. Unlike art, an NFT can't be destroyed, and ownership and provenance are far more easily verifiable. For those doubting the legitimacy or staying power of NFTs one thing is for certain: the market for NFTs is real. A variety of online marketplaces and even famous auction houses like Christies are selling NFTs, often for staggering prices.

In 2021, the total volume of NFT sales averaged over $100 million per month as their popularity and public awareness boomed. Early 2021 attracted an explosion of speculators who anticipate that NFTs today may be like owning a collectible piece of art before the rest of the world knew how good that artist was. NFTs are also unique in the wide diversity of what can become an NFT. Currently, NFT-backed digital items range from brief video clips to video game skins to audiobooks and even tweets (Twitter CEO Jack Dorsey's first tweet sold for $2.9 million as an NFT).

Who Creates NFTs?

Entrepreneurs, art advocates, corporations, and even average Joes and Joannas create NFTs. Many take digital content that they have created or own and mint the NFT that backs it. Minting NFTs has become a practical reality due to the ability to use blockchain technology to create unique products. The Ethereum blockchain is the most common way to build NFTs and is thus the most frequently used cryptocurrency for buying NFTs. For less than $100 in cryptocurrency, many platforms and marketplaces, like OpenSea, Rarible, and Mintable will create an NFT from any type of digital content. This has opened the field to content creators, subjects, and novices to create their own NFTs. No experience is necessary, and as long as someone can prove they created or legally own the content, they can build an NFT. For authors, artists, videographers, social media personalities, video game enthusiasts, and others, creating an NFT from their work can lead to surprisingly high yields when they bring their NFT to the market.

Other NFT creators are entrepreneurs seeking to capitalize on the booming market. Corporations, including professional sports associations, social media companies, and brands like Taco Bell and even Charmin toilet paper are all using NFTs to generate buzz and revenue. Some companies specialize in speculating on NFTs, banking that their value will continue to increase. NFT creators have different motivations, but with user-friendly technology and a thriving market, content makers and businesspeople alike are building their own NFT portfolios. Newspapers are publishing each issue as an NFT and sports collectors are minting NFTs from famous moments in sports history. In the future, it's possible that much of the new content being produced will become NFTs. Like connoisseurs of art, wine, or trading cards, NFT collectors will purchase new NFTs with the hope that demand will increase as that product or creator grows in popularity.

Why Create NFTs?

The 2021 boom in NFTs has coincided with increased popularity and mainstream acceptance of cryptocurrencies. Cryptocurrency supporters see the various types of alternative legal tender as offering huge advantages over traditional fiat currency. NFTs are built using blockchain technology and are typically paid for with cryptocurrency. While volatility continues to be an issue, cryptocurrency prices have skyrocketed in the past three years, as increasing numbers of institutional and retail investors buy into the market. There is also a practical element to creating NFTs that makes them appealing. Using blockchain and cryptocurrency gives NFTs a few advantages over other types of collectibles and entices more content owners to make NFTs:

1. NFTs are almost impossible to forge or counterfeit because each has a unique identifier with its blockchain code.

2. Unlike a piece of art or a rare baseball card, no experts are needed to verify the authenticity and organize a

sale. NFTs can be authenticated and sold entirely in online marketplaces without any middlemen.

3. NFTs are much easier to buy and sell. With nearly instant transfers from remote locations around the world, NFTs are the perfect collectible for the online world.

In addition to creating NFTs to compete with the traditional collectible market and to capitalize on the boom, some creators make NFTs for other, more intrinsic reasons. The internet has made most types of art, music, videos, and writing free for public consumption. NFTs push back on this notion by bringing recognizable and monetizable scarcity and rarity to online content—even if it can be viewed for free.

Bottom Line

The online artist Beeple sold his original art as an NFT for nearly $70 million, demonstrating the high market potential. NFTs are increasingly becoming a common way for online content creators to be recognized and paid for their work. The jury is still out on whether NFTs are a good investment and will maintain their popularity levels over time. Those who mint NFTs are banking on the value of digital assets and tokens as the digital world continues to grow and people want more scarcity and significance, even as free content remains the online norm. For many NFT creators, they represent something even more than a monetary opportunity: NFTs endow value and significance to online content that is all too often taken for granted.

NFTs occupy the unique space at the nexus of intellectual property, commodities, and securities. As such, no regulatory framework has yet been developed, and wrangling continues as various federal and international agencies struggle not only to define NFTs but also to determine appropriate legal jurisdictions for overseeing them. The Securities and Exchange Commission continues to investigate whether some minters and exchanges are using NFTs to raise funds similar to the way companies sell securities. The SEC was particularly focused on fractional NFTs, which to some, look suspiciously similar to shares of stock.

Seller Beware:
Before You Jump on the NFT Bandwagon

While the gold rush might have peaked, public interest in non-fungible tokens (NFTs) continues to grow, and their popularity is increasing. In February, Logan Paul sold over $5 million worth of NFTs in 48 hours, while musician Post

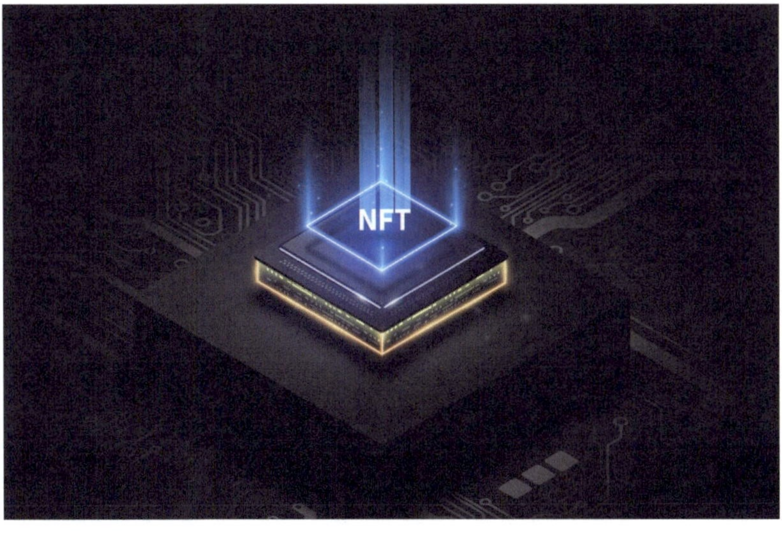

Malone took the unique approach of inviting fans to play beer pong with him if they bought his NFTs.
Given the enormous interest in NFTs and the potential for significant profits from minting, selling, or trading them, any current or aspiring NFT sellers must be familiar with applicable securities laws to avoid running afoul of the Law.

What Exactly are NFTs?
An 'NFT' is a unique certificate of authenticity, created using blockchain technology to document the digital ownership of an underlying physical or digital asset.

NFTs are simple to make through a process known as "minting." While NFTs can be made on virtually any blockchain, the Ethereum blockchain is a popular choice for many NFT sellers. Minters can convert almost anything into an NFT—photographs, paintings, drawings, tweets, music, and more.

Securities Laws and NFTs
NFTs have the potential to disrupt nearly every creative industry. There is enormous profit potential associated with creating and trading NFTs, and securities laws and regulations are struggling to keep pace with rapid technological developments.

Any NFT seller should understand how securities laws affect their business. Failure to comply with securities laws can result in heavy fines from federal and state securities regulators, as well as court injunctions. In the most serious cases, failure to comply with securities laws could result in criminal charges. Consulting a securities lawyer familiar with NFTs and the regulatory framework that governs them is crucial to minimize these risks.

When You Hear "Security," What Comes to Your Mind?
Stocks, bonds, mutual funds, ETFs, and other similar investments, right? While the Securities Act of 1933 specifically exempts tokens and coins (and by extrapolation, virtual or crypto currencies) from the list of regulated securities, it also specifically includes "investment contracts" as subject to regulation. The term is used as a catch-all phrase for any asset that behaves and "feels" like security.

In addition, the U.S. Supreme Court defined an investment contract using a four-part test in the seminal case of *SEC v. Howey* (1946). If an investment checks the below criteria, an investment contract exists:

- Investment in money
- At a common enterprise
- With a reasonable expectation of profit
- Through the efforts of others

The Howey case considers the token's design, issuance, and how it interacts with its platform or blockchain in analyzing whether it meets these four criteria. Despite their uniqueness, tokens share a few common characteristics.

Legal Documents Required for NFT Marketplaces
An NFT marketplace is a platform that connects NFT buyers and sellers. On these platforms, buyers can browse listed assets, buy NFT tokens, and participate in NFT auctions, while sellers can mint NFT tokens with the digital asset they've created. There are several legal considerations and paperwork that must be taken into account before starting an NFT marketplace.

- ***Service Terms And Conditions***—It is critical to have legal documents for use as a contract between the platform operators and its users with clear terms of service. Complete and well-thought-out terms of service agreements can protect a company from a variety of potentially damaging legal issues. An indemnification framework to protect the company is part of this agreement, limiting its overall liability. They are critical in NFT marketplaces due to the high risk of user misconduct.

- ***Policy Concerning Personal Information***—The law requires each business to disclose information about its data collection and use practices. Users can benefit from privacy policies that provide transparency and extend significant peace of mind. Disclosures and other user-determined options should be added depending on the privacy law framework that applies to the business, such as GDPR, CCPA, HIPAA). Marketplace operators can also build trust with their users by implementing privacy policies. Potential customers would be justifiably wary of marketplaces with poorly written privacy policies.

- ***Entity Registration***—Before launching a marketplace, a corporate entity must be established to protect the owners from liability while keeping their assets safe. They equally benefit from a stronger brand image, increasing customer satisfaction.

- ***Community Standards***—NFT marketplaces tend to have a strong user focus due to the high volume of user transactions and user-generated content involved. As such, it is a good idea to include community standards to ensure that user interactions go off without a hitch. They can also give users guidance on how to conduct themselves in the marketplace. By defining their vision, values, and expectations, marketplace operators can build a loyal following for their marketplace.

Other Regulations and Considerations

Given the unique legal challenges posed by NFT marketplaces, other documented policies, both internal and external, may be necessary or otherwise beneficial. External policies can help a company clarify its position on specific actions and behaviors. Internal policies can assist them in implementing and standardizing their organization's response to regulatory issues,, external policies, and other legal obligations should they arise:

Compliance with Securities Law

Each NFT should be examined for compliance based on its unique characteristics while bearing in mind that NFTs that underpin collectibles are not securities. These NFTs are finished goods whose value depends on a direct sale to a customer. NFT issuers must be careful not to sell their NFTs for profit, appreciation, or dividends. An NFT's marketing alone has the potential to turn it from non-security to security. Issuers should avoid, and NFT marketplaces should prevent:

1. Using NFTs as part of a fundraising drive to build a network for upcoming sales

2. Promoting NFTs through sponsorship, promotion, or third parties

3. Promising potential buyers the possibility of capital appreciation for the digital asset or profit from the efforts of the creator or another third party

Content Moderation

All communities and forums need to moderate their content. The chance of a user making an offensive or inappropriate comment is high. But with technical safeguards in place, such infractions can be easily detected, and unwanted content removed.

Authentication

An essential feature of NFTs is their uniqueness, and customers who purchase NFTs expect them to be 100 percent genuine. However, NFTs can be counterfeited, which causes a slew of issues. For example, it is possible for a producer to mint multiple NFTs for the same digital asset by creating exact replicas of other parties' works (e.g., in a similar but different file format, such as MP3 vs. MP4, PNG vs. JPG, etc.) NFT marketplaces should, at the very least, prohibit any behavior that leads to the unlicensed commercialization of underlying works.

Content-related Issue

NFT marketplaces are already overflowing with user-generated content and transactions, and content-related issues surrounding intellectual property rights and licensing are a frequent occurrence. Blockchain technology itself has some limitations that could cause further problems.

NFTs and Legal Complexity — Is it Worth the Hassle?

Non-fungible tokens pose a new set of commercial, regulatory, and legal considerations that are not present with fungible tokens. Regulations and laws in the U.S. are slowly catching up with advancing technology. Among the critical legal issues is the classification of NFTs, intellectual property rights, the implications of money laundering and sanctions, cybersecurity issues, and state laws relating to virtual currencies. Investment In this asset class is evolving, and fintech companies, financial services companies, and investors must consider critical legal issues in this space and plan carefully to take advantage of potential opportunities while avoiding and minimizing areas of significant risk.

While investors hoping to cash in on rising NFT prices must be aware that their profits likely will be taxed as capital gains, sellers, too, run significant financial and regulatory risks when embarking on an NFT fundraising or commercial scheme. Current regulatory and legal precedents governing investments and securities represent the proverbial round hole to NFTs' square peg. Until the SEC, IRS, and the courts come up with an enforceable set of rules designed specifically for NFTs, cryptocurrencies, and other digital assets, buyers and sellers will be flying blind. The danger is that regulators, litigators, and legislators will establish the ground rules only after the players have taken the field.

Phonies, Phishing, & Functionaries: Risks in Buying and Selling NFTs

The market for non-fungible tokens (NFTs) has boomed (and busted) over the past year. As businesses and asset owners continue to create and sell NFTs representing a range of physical assets, digital images, internet memes, event tickets, memorabilia, and more, the legal risks associated with buying

and selling NFTs have come into greater focus than ever. This article outlines these risks and offers proven practices that emerging technologies companies can adopt to protect themselves.

Regulatory Uncertainty Reigns

One of the biggest legal risks surrounding NFTs is the uncertainty surrounding the legislative context in which NFTs exist. While certain aspects or features of NFTs may be regulated by existing laws, there is currently no uniform regulatory framework pertaining to NFTs in the US.

For example, if the Securities and Exchange Commission and other regulators determine that a specific NFT has the characteristics of a security, they may classify it as such under the Securities Act 1933 and the Securities Exchange Act 1934.

On the other hand, NFTs could be considered commodities under the Commodity Exchange Act (CEA), which defines the term to include several enumerated items and a catch-all for "all other goods and articles." The Commodity Futures Trading Commission (CFTC) is on record as saying the definition applies to cryptocurrencies like Bitcoin and Ether, as well as renewable energy credits, emission allowances, and other fungible items. From a recipient, buyer, or investor's perspective, it is unclear whether they would receive any protection from the US law or regulatory policy.

In addition, the ownership of the underlying digital asset that an NFT represents may bring the NFT's copyright into question. The absence of a coherent legal framework for NFTs elevates any potential risk associated with buying and selling them. Buying NFTs might be particularly risky from a consumer welfare point of view, as lawmakers and regulators are concerned about protecting vulnerable and naive populations.

Counterfeit Products and Trademark Infringement

Another legal risk related to buying and selling NFTs pertains to counterfeit products and trademark infringement. The immense popularity of NFTs has increased incidents of cyber fraud in the market. In numerous cases, spoofs of original NFT stores have been launched on the internet. These fake marketplaces utilize the defrauded site's branding, content, and legal documentation, such as terms and conditions and privacy policy, to make them appear authentic. These fake NFT stores exist to sell bogus NFTs to which they either have not secured the intellectual property rights to reproduce or that do not even exist in the real world. This creates massive risk for emerging technologies companies who purchase NFTs for use in games, extended reality content, or virtual meta worlds.

Cybersecurity Risks

Hacking, phishing, brute-force attacks, and social engineering that plague online communities also present a worrying threat to buyers and sellers of NFTs. Hackers are using these and other techniques to convince individuals to willingly transfer their NFTs from their wallets. It is important to clarify that although NFTs exist on the blockchain, the key to unlocking the block and using and transferring the NFT is housed in wallets. In other words, even though it might be possible to track down stolen NFTs, it is generally difficult to recover them.

Loss or Damage to the Physical Asset

Another risk associated with NFTs is related to the loss or damage of the physical asset to which it is tied. Generally, the NFT and its underlying asset are separate assets. An NFT could be rendered worthless if the underlying asset is destroyed, lost, or stolen, even though the NFT generally includes the NFT holder's title to the NFT. Owners of NFTs tied wine and liquor are forewarned. Dropping, partaking from, or even simply uncorking the bottle could affect the NFT's worth.

Take Steps to Protect Yourself

- ***Appropriate Legal Documentation***
  Every NFT project should have a certain set of documents that includes terms and conditions, a privacy policy, and a license agreement. If you are a seller, make sure that you have these documents for your NFT project. If you are a buyer, read these documents carefully as they should outline what you are purchasing. In any case, it is best to engage an NFT attorney to review the documents before signing an agreement to buy or sell.

- ***Legal Due-Diligence***
  Beyond a document review, it is often worthwhile to conduct due diligence to ensure the legitimacy of any transaction, especially if a large financial transfer is involved. Companies might be tempted to conduct their own research or perform a perfunctory background check themselves but there is a risk of missing out on important details as the catch usually lies in the details. Many law firms specialize in conducting due diligence for NFT-related transactions; engaging these experts can help avoid extremely costly or damaging situations.

- ***Reputable Dealers and Services***
  Given the cybersecurity concerns, it is important to follow some best practices when buying and selling NFTs. These include but are not limited to setting up a reputable crypto wallet, safely storing the wallet's private keys, installing anti-virus software, and enabling two-factor

authentication. To mitigate the risks of purchasing NFTs, buyers should ideally make sure that they trade only on reputable marketplaces, research what they are actually purchasing, and check that the related smart contracts accurately match the terms related to the transaction.

Conclusion

NFTs offer exciting opportunities for digital creators, sellers, and buyers alike. As the market continues to evolve, it is crucial that market participants fully understand the risks inherent in these products. To minimize exposure, buyers and sellers should consult an NFT attorney before transacting NFTs, as timely advice can help mitigate potentially significant legal risks. Among other things, an NFT attorney can be helpful in conducting legal due diligence, drafting legal documents, and advising on the regulatory regime applicable to NFT transactions.

Less than three weeks after this March 2022 article was published, the Ninth Circuit Court reaffirmed the first sale doctrine in Bluetooth SIG Inc. v. FCA US LLC. *While the case did not address NFT sales specifically, the court did hold that first sale applies "when a trademarked product has been incorporated in a new product." The ruling could bear on cases such as Nike vs. StockX (see our article in this book) though the Ninth Circuit's affirmation specifically exempts a purchaser of intellectual property who does no more than stock, display, and resell a producer's product under the producer's trademark.*

Royalty Treatment: Does the Resale Right Apply to NFTs?

An artist resale royalty, or *droit de suite* as it is often called in Europe, provides artists with an opportunity to benefit from the increased value of their works over time by granting them a percentage of the proceeds from the resale of their original works of art.

The royalty originated in France in the 1920s and is in general practice throughout Europe but is not part of United States copyright law. Instead, under the first sale doctrine, 17 U.S.C. § 109, the lawful owner of a copyrighted work may "sell or otherwise dispose of the possession of that copy" and "display that copy publicly..." all without the author's permission., Thus, a purchased painting, sculpture, or another piece of art may be treated like a house, car, or any other possession.

Much of the value of NFT art for minters and artists who digitize and list their works lies in proceeds from resales as values rise. Determining whether the resale right, the first sale doctrine, a combination of the two, or some other legal concept should apply will significantly affect the industry's economic vitality. This article will examine the place of the resale right and first sale doctrine with regard to NFT artwork and the use of tokens in video game development.

A Deeper Dive into Resale Rights and NFTs

The resale right affords artists protection against their works being sold too cheaply. It works by giving the creator a slice of the proceeds each time the work is resold and allowing them to participate along with collectors and speculators in the items' appreciation. , The right of resale originated during the explosion of cultural creativity known as the *années folles* (crazy times) that engulfed France in the 1920s, and it is established policy throughout Europe. Current US copyright law, however, does not recognize the resale right, although numerous attempts have been made to incorporate it into federal legislation. When artists sell NFTs of their work, a typical sales agreement would include a mechanism that allows them to receive royalties not only on the original sale but also on ensuing resales. Blockchain smart contracts track payment transactions and distribute royalties to the artists.

The resale right comes into play in video game companies because NFTs are increasingly used as in-game assets that players can earn through gameplay, trades, and third-party sales. Common practice is for game companies to create NFT assets as work-for-hire or work products and retain the resale rights for themselves, earning ongoing revenues for rare and high-utility items. However, game companies that purchase rights to creative assets can arrange for the artists to receive passive income as players sell the related skins, weapons, virtual real estate, and collector's cards over the course of gameplay or trade on secondary markets. However, since the US copyright law does not recognize resale rights, it is unclear whether any provision regarding royalties under the smart contract would apply to video game companies operating in the US.

A Second Look at First Sale

US copyright law does not recognize resale rights but instead stipulates that once an original copyright-protected work of authorship is sold, the buyer and all subsequent purchasers are free to resell that work without compensating the original artist or author. This first sale principle is the exact opposite of the resale right. However, successive judicial decisions have held that the first sale doctrine does not apply to digital works. For example, in *Capitol Records LLC v. ReDigi Inc.*, the US Court of Appeals for the Second Circuit held that the first sale doctrine does not apply to digital music files because the resale would require making an unauthorized copy of the digital music file which would infringe upon the copyright owner's reproduction right. Similarly, in *Disney Enterprises Inc. v. Redbox Automated Retail LLC*, the US District Court for Central California held that the first sale doctrine did not apply to digital download codes because the sale of movie download codes essentially granted the ability to create physical copies at some point in the future rather than a particular, fixed copy of a copyrighted work.

Based on the existing precedent, it would seem that the first sale doctrine does not apply to NFTs tied to digital objects such as audio files and digital images. In other words, the right to sell or distribute the digital version of a work, be it a drawing, digital music file, or photograph, belongs exclusively to the copyright owner. However, it is generally in the copyright owner's interest to allow the resale because a limited form of contracting might be possible: while US copyright law does not recognize the resale right, the NFT sales agreement can be written such that the seller is obligated to pay royalties to the copyright owner if the in-game asset is sold to a third party. Moreover, these provisions can be executed by smart contracts to ensure they are accurately and consistently applied every time that a sale occurs. In these cases, it is in the copyright owners' interest to allow resales, as they will receive resale royalties under the terms of the NFT sales agreement.

Further, it is unlikely that the first sale doctrine will apply to cases where a lawful digital artwork owner attempts the unauthorized minting of an in-game digital asset or NFT. Since "ownership" of digital artwork is more akin to possessing a license to access the work than actual ownership of a particular copy, the right to convert the artwork into an NFT resides solely with the copyright owner. In cases where the lawful owner of a physical artwork attempts to mint an NFT without the consent of the copyright owner, the outcome will likely be the same.

Conclusion

The surge in popularity and usage of digital assets such as NFTs and murkiness surrounding the application of the first sale doctrine may force courts to draft a first sale doctrine that specifically addresses these use cases. In the meantime, the first sale doctrine is unlikely to be applicable to the sale of

NFTs. This is because when a buyer purchases an in-game NFT, they would acquire a link to a digital version of the asset the NFT represents. This acts as an option to create a copy of the digital work, and US courts currently do not acknowledge a first sale doctrine for digital works. Nevertheless, a limited form of contracting of royalty provisions in the NFT sales agreement might be possible. It is best to consult an attorney specializing in copyright, contracts, and NFTs for guidance on this complex issue.

Unlike the traditional collectible art market, NFT artists can reap a share of the rewards as their creations are resold for higher and higher prices. Artists can guarantee these passive income streams by structuring smart contracts that automatically direct royalties based on the resale price directly to their accounts. For an expanded discussion of how these "commissions" apply, read Royalty Treatment: Does the Resale Right Apply to NFTs? in this section of the book. Engaging an agent and an attorney can ensure both the artist and the NFT minter's rights are protected, and the agreement language is clear with respect to each party's rights and responsibilities.

Mint Conditions: NFT Artist Agreements

Legal issues arising from intellectual property-related concerns have received wide coverage in recent months and, in some cases, have derailed popular NFT projects. It's no exaggeration to say that the success of an NFT project may hinge on how well the NFT artist agreement is drafted and how well it defines the terms under which an NFT minter can

use any underlying art. This article covers the main ingredients in a strong NFT artist agreement and some important points that NFT minters and artists must know to protect their rights.

Meaning and Importance of an NFT Artist Agreement

An NFT artist agreement is a legal document that outlines the terms and conditions under which the creator of an original work—a piece of art, music, consumer good, or another type of intellectual property—grants certain rights to the minter of an NFT based on that work in exchange for compensation. Artists very reasonably seek to protect their work (irrespective of the medium) from unauthorized reproduction and sale and to participate in their commercialization. An NFT artist agreement is the equivalent of a license agreement used in traditional or digital media to say, produce and sell T-shirts emblazoned with a sports team logo or a cartoon mouse. It defines the scope of the grant of license in advance, reducing the likelihood of conflict or disputes between the NFT minter and the artist. The agreement may be called a non-fungible token digital art commission contract, commission agreement for NFT artwork, NFT digital artist commission agreement, digital art agreement, artist commission agreement, licensing agreement, or another similar term.

If NFT minters or developers fail to obtain a signed NFT artist agreement before creating an NFT based on artwork they do not own, they may be inviting conflicts down the road pertaining to the underlying asset's copyright, trademark, or other intellectual property rights. For example, recently, an art collector has filed a lawsuit before a New York federal court to clarify rights over celebrated Indian artist M.F. Husain's painting, *Lightning* or *The Guernica of India*. The art collector purchased the 60-foot mural and plans to sell NFTs based on it. The artist's estate objected, claiming that buying the painting does not convey the rights necessary to carry out the plan. Because the purchase agreement makes no mention of NFT rights, there is no clear way to assess each party's position on what actually changed hands when the collector bought the piece.

Key Provisions in NFT Artist Agreements

A strong, comprehensive NFT artist agreement will delineate the arrangement's scope, each party's rights and obligations, the working relationship between parties, timelines and deadlines, copyright ownership, and more:

- ***Scope of the Agreement***—At a minimum, the NFT artist agreement should clearly describe the artwork being licensed or purchased, the duration of the license, what fee, royalties, or other consideration the artist will receive in exchange for signing the contract, and what the licensor is allowed to do with the NFTs he or she creates.

- ***Relationship Between Parties***—In many cases, an NFT minter will simply commission artwork from artists on a work-for-hire basis. In this scenario, the minter would be considered a commissioning agent or commissioning party while the artist serves as a contractor who produces a product that will be owned by the minter. In other situations, a company might use in-house illustrators or graphic artists who produce works to be minted into NFTs. In this situation, the employer-employee relationship takes precedence. The worker would have no more right to the NFT than an assembly line worker to a car she helps build. Other cases are not so cut and dry. IP owners and artists may engage a third party to produce NFTs based on their owned works and display, market, sell, or otherwise leverage them in various partnership arrangements. These may include advance payments, royalty splits, profit sharing, options, and other sophisticated deals best drawn up by an experienced NFT attorney.

- ***Rights and Obligations***—The license should explain any obligations the artist, the NFT minter, and any future purchaser of the NFTs created must perform and the compensation they will receive. Agreements commonly spell out whether the artist is allowed to make physical or digital copies of the artwork, license the artwork to other parties, and receive royalties for the original and/or subsequent sales of NFTs based on the artwork. Similarly, the agreement should stipulate whether the minter can retain exclusive rights to the NFT for a certain period of time, determine its sale price, or sub-license the rights granted. The artist's obligations may include the duty to produce high-quality artwork, deliver it in a timely manner, and ensure that the rights of any third party are not infringed in its production. The contract should lay out how and when the NFT minter will pay the artist and may require attribution of the work to the artist or author at all times and maintain the spirit of the art and reputation of the artist in any derivative works.

- ***Copyright***—Copyright ownership can cause significant issues when not sufficiently defined in an NFT artist agreement. The courts have decided that copyright to underlying assets does not automatically transfer to NFT minters, purchasers, and licensees. The artist retains the right to transfer the copyright, grant a license for specific purposes, or limit the use of NFTs. If the intent of the minter is for the artist to convey any of these rights, it must be expressly stated in the NFT artist agreement. If not, the artist who created the original artwork retains the copyright.

- ***Jurisdiction***—With NFT legislation still in its infancy and each state and country creating regulations and setting precedents within their borders, it is recommended that the NFT artist agreement specify which jurisdiction will rule should any disagreement arise. Some jurisdictions are proving to be sympathetic to NFT minters, while others tend to side with artists. The country in which the artist lives or the licensing company is incorporated may play a role, giving one side a "home field advantage."

- ***Liability***—Since the rules surrounding NFTs are still evolving, it is important for the NFT artist agreement to include a clause laying out the consequences each party will face should they fail to deliver on their obligations. These consequences should take into account that the failure may be the result of forces beyond their control. For example, a jurisdiction may pass new regulatory controls that make minting NFTs more difficult or even illegal; natural disasters may destroy the means for creating the artwork or minting the NFT.

Any business or individual intending to create, sell, mint, or develop NFTs should always protect their rights and clarify their responsibilities by creating and entering into an NFT artist agreement with their artist partners. It is best to hire an attorney experienced in NFTs and contract law to draft the NFT artist agreement as they can be complex documents. It is important to note that many NFT artist agreements fail to adequately safeguard the interests of both parties, as they are drafted either by artist advocacy groups or NFT minter proponents.

The early days of NFT investing have been based on speculation rather than any rational belief that a digital gorilla cartoon or pixelated Punk will suddenly achieve critical acclaim or viral popularity. Since most NFTs carry no intrinsic benefits, their value is determined simply by how much someone is willing to pay for them. Most financial professionals advise investing in NFTs only for fun, using discretionary funds, similar to "investing" in a lottery ticket. Most NFTs are illiquid, and despite their rising popularity draw a limited pool of potential buyers. The tips contained in this essay are even more pertinent than when it was written, given the "crypto winter" of mid-2022.

Bulls and Bears and Apes, Oh My! Investing in NFTs

Interest in non-fungible tokens, commonly referred to as NFTs, reached an all-time high over the past year. NFTs are commonly produced from digital art, collectibles, fantasy and esports, static images, memes, video clips, audio files, and a growing number of other media. These use cases are trendy

and potentially lucrative, luring many celebrities and social media influencers into minting, investing, and promoting NFTs on their social media feeds. Bored Ape Yacht Club's owners include Snoop Dogg, Tom Brady, Shaquille O'Neal, Serena Williams, Justin Bieber, and Kevin Hart, to mention but a few. This interest among athletes and A-listers also added fuel to the spark of interest among both institutional and retail investors.

NFT Risks – What Investors Should Know

Art NFTs can be volatile investments because their worth is highly subjective, based as much on their viral reputation as their artistic content. It's a fickle market, and value can skyrocket and bottom out within days. Non-high net-worth individuals considering a plunge into NFT investing should note that information on NFTs circulates very differently from that of stocks. One can learn about stocks through market research, brokerage firms, and overall industry trends.

Unlike stocks, however, public understanding of NFTs is based largely on social media posts, trends, and word of mouth. Not all of it is reliable, and it is often unevenly distributed and incomplete.

Additionally, because the NFT market is so new, some financial advisors have cautioned their clients to steer clear of NFT investing altogether. Some suggest purchasing NFTs for fun only, rather than their appreciation potential. In other words, don't bet the house or the kids' college fund on a flying cat or an ennui-plagued primate. NFTs should not be relied upon for passive income or building retirement funds. Many financial strategists recommend diverse investment portfolios that allocate less than 5 percent in total to NFTs and never let that investment get in the way of other long-term financial goals.

Best Practices for Investing in NFTs

If you decide that the potential reward is worth the risk, here are some best practices for NFT investments:

- ***Conduct Your Own Research***: Thoroughly research the NFT investments that you are interested in. Research their team, trade history, set up, execution, social engagement numbers, artwork, originality, and rarities to best make informed decisions.

- ***Carefully Vet the Seller***: Be sure to perform background research on the person or organization offering the NFT for sale. This is crucial because many celebrities and NFT creators have attracted impersonators who try to sell fake NFTs. Indeed, numerous celebrities and NFT creators have participated in NFT projects that turned out to be complete scams. Learn as much as you can about the seller as humanly possible. Search OpenSea, Foundation, or Rarible, which are the most common NFT markets. Other niche marketplaces exist that specialize in specific types of assets. Also, research niche marketplaces that specialize in the type of NFT that you are interested in.

- ***Mind the Middle Ground***: High-visibility NFT projects are often expensive, inaccessible, and overpriced. Low-end projects are much easier to get into but have limited traction or potential for financial gains. It is best to mind the middle ground when it comes to investing in NFTs.

- ***Create a Digital Wallet***: This is a place where you can 'store' your NFTs and cryptocurrency tokens. Various types of cryptowallets exist, but arguably the best method of storage is to spread your crypto assets across different types.

- ***Fund Your Account***: You will need to connect your bank account or credit card to an exchange to purchase or trade cryptocurrencies. Know Your Customer (KYC) and Anti-money Laundering (AML) requirements vary from jurisdiction to jurisdiction, and this may include an identity verification process. Always protect yourself by correctly completing the identity verification process.

- ***Negotiate Terms:*** Depending on what's being sold, deals could include upfront payouts or a royalty on all future sales.

- ***Guard Against Theft and Fraud***: Because crypto is difficult to trace, has no central controlling authority, and is internationally accessible, there are potentially large security risks involving user data, crypto, and passwords. Even cash transactions can be compromised. Purchasing cyber liability insurance is one expensive option to minimize theft and fraud. Other ways to prevent theft and fraud include common-sense strategies such as using strong and unique passwords, never (ever!) sharing your keys, avoiding public networks and WIFI, using crypto hardware wallets, and not storing anything in the cloud. Another key point is to review and validate every app and crypto exchange you use for security features and reputation.

- ***Do Not Infringe on Intellectual Property Rights***: Remember that the original NFT creators typically retain the copyright. Thus, buyers and investors own only the specific digital/physical copy that they purchased and the right to display depictions of that copy, unless a creative commons license applies or there is an express transfer of the underlying ownership in the terms and conditions governing the NFT. Intellectual property rights can get complicated. If you are specifically seeking intellectual property rights, you should consult with an attorney who can provide reliable advice.

- ***Consider the Tax Implications*:** The IRS currently views crypto tokens as property and not currency, but one thing is clear: NFTs are subject to capital gains tax. But they may not receive the preferential long-term capital gains rates that stocks enjoy. NFTs may even be taxed at a higher collectibles tax rate.

- ***Consult Experts*:** Always engage an attorney, accountant, or financial planner to assist in understanding both the short-term and long-term risks and impacts of your NFT investments. Gamma Law, a San Francisco-based law firm, has been at the forefront of blockchain, cryptocurrency, and NFT market trends. Gamma Law attorneys specialize in providing sound legal advice for NFT investments.

Despite the popularity of NFT investing, tokens remain, overall, a volatile asset class and are often saddled with high mark-ups, brokerage charges, and other fees. Still, many high-net-worth investors are willing to take the financial risk associated with investing in NFTs. According to a recent worldwide poll conducted by DeVere, out of 450 clients, 26 percent reported the desire to add NFT investments to their portfolios by the end of the 2022 fiscal year. However, as crypto investor Sina Estavi recently discovered, high-value NFTs don't always maintain their value. In 2021, Estavi bought the NFT of Jack Dorsey's first tweet for $2.9 million;

when he listed it for sale in April 2022, bids failed to reach $14,000. The moral of the story: investors should prepare themselves for the possibility they will lose the money invested in NFTs.

If you are considering investing in NFTs, it is wise to consult an attorney experienced in the space to understand how the discussion above may impact you and your investments.

Crypto and blockchain fans naturally took exception to Bill Gates' assertion that the big 2021 run-up in the price of many NFTs was simply a manifestation of the greater fool theory. Time will tell which side is correct, but Gates seems to have overlooked several utilitarian uses for the tokens. For instance, a Miami law firm created an NFT of court documents to serve individuals suspected of using the anonymity of the blockchain to commit fraud and theft. While NFTs currently may not "improve the world immensely," as Gates states, they do contribute in small ways to a better society by serving as title deeds, content gatekeepers, allowing access to member benefits, and more.

Poor (or Rich?) Little Fool?
NFTs and the Greater Fool Theory

Non-fungible tokens (NFTs) have exploded in popularity since the development of the blockchain. While NFTs are mostly created for art, sports collectibles, virtual real estate, or other in-game assets, they are unique, indivisible tokens registered on the Ethereum blockchain that give them unique

fingerprints that cannot be replicated or altered. Powered by smart contracts that tie them to an owner at all times, the blocks on a chain are visible to the public and enable NFT creators to retain their intellectual property rights and royalties. They've changed the game for the digital content realm and power a new economy, one in which people with extra money to spend want to participate.

Eight-figure price tags and celebrity endorsements have driven the general public toward NFTs and pushed NFTs toward the mainstream. In 2021, the global NFT market value topped an estimated $15.70 billion and is expected to reach $122.43 billion by 2028. Yet, some savvy businesspeople aren't convinced. Bill Gates, for instance, recently described the rise of NFTs as being based on the "Greater Fool Theory." He doesn't think buying NFTs of bored monkeys or yesterday's tweets will last because they won't help the world. Gates describes himself as an old-school investor who won't invest in cryptocurrencies since they aren't a protected asset class. While his concerns have some merit, NFTs do boast many willing buyers and sellers, with many playing for high stakes.

Chain of Fools

The market has experienced two significant bubbles over the past 20 years—the real estate crash in the 2000s and the tech-stock bubble in the late 1990s. A market bubble forms when a series of assets increase in price dramatically beyond their fundamental value. Tulip bulbs, anyone? Investments are allocated to purchase these overpriced assets, contravening what, in hindsight, seem to be prudent strategies. No one really knows how a market bubble forms or what causes prices to continue to rise until the bubble bursts., One popular theory that describes this phenomenon is known as the Greater Fool Theory.

According to economists, the Greater Fool Theory takes hold when people can find buyers to whom to sell overinflated assets. These people buy the stock, commodity, or collectible without regard to its intrinsic value because accumulating value is not their objective. Profit is. And they can always find a bigger fool than they are who will pay more than they did. The bubble bursts when the "greatest fool" buys the item and is left holding the bag. This investing ignores all valuations, earnings reports, and any other market data. As long as there is a greater fool in the market, there is no need for prudence, so speculators can safely ignore the asset's fundamentals.

Fool's Gold?

As applied to the NFT marketplace, cryptocurrency markets dipped significantly in the spring and summer of 2022, thanks in part due to the TerraUSD crash, but will NFTs suffer the same fate? Perhaps not. Many stakeholders, Bill Gates notwithstanding, view NFTs as valuable investments because they verify the authenticity of the asset they represent, unlike an oil painting or a baseball card. With the rising popularity of digital images, the technology available makes it easy to copy a Caravaggio or counterfeit a Campanella. There's nothing to authenticate whether you own an Old Master or a master forgery.

Smart contracts, on the other hand, allow NFT creators to identify their works and NFT owners to verify that their NFTs are indeed "original" pieces of digital art or collectibles. NFTs become digital versions of these collectibles, whether the underlying asset takes the form of wine, baseball card, film clip, event ticket, or something else. NFTs have ushered in a whole new marketplace for digital creations.

The technology behind NFTs—the tokens registered on the blockchain—authorizes them to protect all parties to any transaction. The seller knows the asset's market value, and the buyer understands he or she is buying a legitimate, unique object. For example, many NFTs have other items tied to them as part of the purchase, such as a concert ticket or a weapon that can be used in a video game. When a concertgoer buys an NFT-based ticket on OpenSea, they will know it will gain them admittance to their show—peace of mind that does not come when buying from Craig's List or a scalper. Likewise, gamers can purchase an NFT gaming asset such as a magic spell or character skin on the game platform from a trusted third-party site. When they decide to stop playing, they can then sell the NFT gaming asset to someone else or swap it for a different one for another game. So, NFTs have an authenticity with their place on the blockchain that other "collectibles" lack, which can arguably remove the "fool" from the Greater Fool Theory.

What a Fool Believes

Despite warnings about "fool" purchases, NFTs are an emerging asset class that will pique the interest of more investors in the future. While they aren't considered securities by the Securities and Exchange Commission (SEC) because they don't meet the "Howey test" guidelines, NFTs straddle the line between categorization as a product and a security.

Currently, the SEC doesn't view NFTs as a security because they concluded NFTs fail the third prong of the Howey test—a reasonable expectation of profits derived from the efforts of others. But this designation may change in the future. NFT creators who consider their assets as products rather than investments but then market them based on their capital gains potential could be courting regulatory trouble. NFT creators can write conditions into their smart contracts stipulating that they receive a portion of the sale price each time it's sold, generating passive income for artists. Within the smart contract, however, there is no expectation that the NFT will make money for the buyer. If the NFT value increases, that is due to the marketplace and not due to any expectation of profit upon its sale like security does. The SEC has greater concerns over fractional NFTs that allow many investors to own a piece of the NFT. Lawsuits, such as a class action against Dapper Labs and an SEC case against a former OpenSea employee for wire fraud and money laundering, have arisen over this very issue.

Although NFTs are not considered securities because they are not divisible or “fungible.” Fractional NFTs, however, blur the line, with some in the SEC viewing them as tantamount to shares in a company. Over time, the SEC has changed its legal purview to regulate other digital assets, and NFTs may be next. NFTs do hold significant value for many owners and creators despite the misgivings of old-school investors and their claim of the Greater Fool Theory that props up their value. While NFTs are more akin to a signed soccer jersey or an original oil painting, they do have intrinsic value that isn’t attributed to the Greater Fool Theory. The SEC has certainly taken notice.

Just as boomtowns sprung up in the Sacramento Valley to "mine the miners" during the 1850s, the NFT gold rush of the 2020s has seen marketplaces emerge to mine the minters and investors. Developing a marketplace to bring together the creators, sellers, and purchasers of digital art, music, videos, collectibles, in-game items, and other assets may prove more lucrative and less risky than active participation in the NFT trade. Entrepreneurs intent on creating marketplaces, however, must exercise sound judgment. Crossing the legal T's and dotting the regulatory I's is critical to creating a community that instills trust, patronage, and profit.

Key Legal Considerations in Building An NFT Marketplace

Non-fungible tokens (NFTs) are becoming increasingly popular. In comparison with fungible tokens such as Bitcoin and Ethereum which can be divided into smaller parts, each non-fungible token is indivisible and has its own distinct value. NFTs can be attached to various digital items, including videos, audio recordings, trading cards, digital art,

and animation. NFTs confirm the ownership of the respective digital items by recording the details of transactions in a digital ledger called a blockchain. Because the ledger is public and distributed over numerous Internet-connected computers, it cannot be destroyed or altered.

Thanks to over-the-top media attention and growing interest from investors, NFTs can have astronomical prices. For example, in March 2021, the BBC reported that an NFT related to a digital artwork was sold at Christie's auction house for $69 million. Taking into account the rising value of NFTs, entrepreneurs may consider launching new NFT marketplaces. However, due to the recent introduction of NFTs (the first NFT was created in 2014), there is still much legal uncertainty regarding the regulation of NFT platforms.

Investors and entrepreneurs interested in creating NFT marketplaces should consider their legal responsibilities and the ramifications of still-developing regulation. Dotting the legal i's and crossing the t's is essential to create, operate, and profit from an NFT marketplace successfully and sustainably. This article provides a guide to the major issues involved.

Documentation

NFT marketplaces must have at least two essential documents in place to protect their operators from legal headaches. Terms of service govern the relationships between the NFT marketplace operator and its customers as well as the relationships between the buyers and sellers of the NFTs featured on the platform. An attorney who is well-versed in contracts, end-user license agreements, and digital technology can draft terms that will stand up to legal challenges and scrutiny. Well-drafted terms decrease the chance of disputes arising between the NFT marketplace and its users. Furthermore, your terms can minimize or eliminate your liability in case of disputes between buyers and sellers. The terms should include provisions for how any disputes arising out of or in relation to the terms will be resolved. Arbitration can be a cost-effective and discrete method of dispute resolution and may facilitate reaching an agreement without the potential reputational damage of public litigation. Your lawyer can advise on whether binding or non-binding arbitration or some other dispute resolution method would be more advantageous in your situation.

As the operator of an NFT marketplace, you will likely process your customers' personal data in order to allow them to conduct payment transactions. Keeping that data safe and secure is a critical task. Many jurisdictions require processors of personal data to clearly disclose their practices in a privacy policy. The fines for privacy violations can be devastating. In 2019, the US Federal Trade Commission (FTC) imposed a $5 billion penalty on Facebook for violating consumers' privacy. An infringement of the EU General Data Protection Regulation (GDPR) may lead to a fine of €20 million or 4 percent of the infringer's worldwide annual revenue, whichever is higher.

In addition to terms of services and a privacy policy, NFT marketplaces displaying, or selling user-generated content may add an additional layer of protection in the form of community guidelines. These guidelines can embed the values of the NFT marketplace in the minds of its users and can be used as a basis to identify and terminate the accounts of users who violate those values such as by posting racist, sexist, homophobic, or otherwise negative content.

Intellectual Property Protection

For an NFT marketplace to operate smoothly, it is necessary to verify and safeguard proper intellectual property rights for each participant through each step of every NFT transaction. For example, the owner of a piece of digital content may need to provide the operator of the NFT marketplace with the rights to publish the digital content in digital galleries, catalogs, compilations of work, and other promotional materials. Without such rights, the NFT marketplace may be unable to provide the services required by buyers and sellers. On the other hand, if the NFT marketplace demands NFT creators and owners cede overly generous rights to their content to the NFT marketplace or other third parties, IP owners may be reluctant to use the NFT marketplace, limiting the operator's effectiveness. An IP and licensing contract attorney with experience in digital technology sectors can ensure a fair allocation of intellectual property rights.

Securities Laws and Regulations

The United States and other countries are exploring how best to regulate transactions involving NFTs. Like art, fine wine, and other collectibles, many NFTs possess aesthetic as well as monetary value, which has caused some jurisdictions to struggle to decide whether to treat them as securities similar to stocks, bonds, and options. Although in many cases NFTs may not constitute securities, certain types of NFTs may fall within the scope of the securities legislation. If an NFT marketplace deals with securities, it may be required to register as a broker-dealer of securities and comply with all applicable securities-related requirements, including those of the US Securities and Exchange Commission (SEC) and any relevant self-regulatory organizations.

NFT marketplaces can take steps to deflect SEC scrutiny and penalties by focusing on NFTs' aesthetic qualities and utility rather than their resale value and potential to appreciate. A rigorous legal analysis of NFTs traded through an NFT marketplace may help its operators avoid sanctions for violating the applicable securities regulations which may include jail sentences.

Consumer Protection

Most major jurisdictions have adopted laws to protect consumers who purchase goods or services. In the US, for example, the Federal Trade Commission Act prohibits deceptive or unfair advertising in any medium. An advertisement is likely to be deceptive if it misleads consumers and affects their decisions, opinions, or behavior about buying a product or service. An advertisement will be considered unfair if it causes or is likely to cause an injury that is substantial, not outweighed by other benefits, and not reasonably avoidable.

If an NFT marketplace fails to adequately inform its customers about what they are purchasing and the risks involved, the FTC may argue that the operator of the NFT marketplace is engaged in deceptive or unfair advertising. This may lead to hefty fines.

Taxation

In general, the US Internal Review Services (IRS) considers NFTs to be "property" and, therefore, anyone engaged in their purchase and sale may be required to pay sales tax and capital gains taxes. NFT marketplaces, therefore, should have in place mechanisms for collecting and remitting sales tax and accurately documenting sale prices, commissions, and other fees. To date, no state tax authority has explicitly acknowledged that NFTs are subject to sales and use tax. Nevertheless, some states have built-in legal frameworks that are sufficiently broad to encompass.

NFTs offer exciting opportunities for a broad range of participants, including marketplace facilitators. As with any business venture in an emerging market, is prudent to perform due diligence to weigh the potential benefits against market, opportunity, and legal risks.

Whether they are simply bowing to anti-token gamers or taking a more conservative approach owing to the cratering of NFT values throughout 2022, many gaming shops have put the development of NFT games and their introduction into established titles and platforms on hold. The NFT bust and crypto winter have also depressed the use of blockchain in the video gaming world. Many observers, however, are bullish on blockchain's role in gaming as a medium for engaging the creator community and expect its resurgence as the economy as a whole bounces back. Ethereum has mitigated the environmental concerns mentioned in this article, reducing energy consumption by 99 percent since "The Merge" in late 2022.

N(o) F(reaking) T(hanks): The Backlash against NFTs in Video Games

Video games are historically a driving factor in the development of new technologies. When the crypto-based assets known as non-fungible tokens (NFTs) first arrived, video game developers embraced them with lightning speed. In what seemed like overnight, many PC and console-based

video games announced they would incorporate NFTs into their platforms to expand the gaming universe and increase revenues. At first blush, it was an interesting and novel idea. Unique active wallets in blockchain gaming grew by 2,000 percent and won $2.5 billion in investment over the 12 months ending in March 2022. Gamers seemed intrigued by the opportunity to purchase NFTs to improve their in-game characters with skins, tools, and other items, but opposition arose shortly after NFTs began appearing in games. This increasingly vocal opposition continues to push back against gaming companies for even announcing plans to plug NFTs into games.

So, What Happened?

Some gamers became incensed at the idea that NFTs would force them to pay to unlock features they believe should be included with the price of the game purchase. Others maintained that grinding for the resources required to obtain in-game NFTs would rob many games of their fun. Many players view the incorporation of NFTs into video games as yet another predatory attempt by gaming companies to squeeze more money out of players. They clashed with Ubisoft, Square Enix, Zynga, and other major game developers over the introduction of NFTs and crypto into their favorite titles.

Many gaming companies, on the other hand, view NFTs as a means for verifying digital assets on the blockchain, conveying proof of ownership that players can sell for a profit in online marketplaces. Gaming companies claim that incorporating NFTs into the games helps build community and "play to earn" opportunities and take the position that NFTs support game players and NFT artists. Many gamers remain unconvinced, especially those still smarting from bad experiences with downloadable content (DLC) or loot boxes. Despite game companies' attempts to draw distinctions by citing blockchain benefits and resale values, an extremely vocal contingent of gamers remains steadfast (this is very much reminiscent of the situation surrounding World of Warcraft in the early 2000s).

NFTs can offer exclusive in-game assets or highly sought-after items, making them potentially worth thousands of dollars and well out of reach of the average gamer. Far from democratizing and making gaming more inclusive, NFTs might reward players who can afford to "pay-to-win," making the playing field more unequal than ever before. Further, some game enthusiasts fear the introduction of valuable NFTs could cause the price of games to increase dramatically, excluding even more potential players from the "community" and diluting the experience.

As if this weren't enough, gamers have expressed significant concerns over scams, thefts, and hacks targeting NFTs and their owners. Illegal activities, such as those that launder money, surround some NFT transactions. The gaming industry is already a breeding ground for fraud, and many gamers believe NFTs will only further attract the worst elements of society. The NFT marketplace isn't regulated strictly, so the threat of gamers being cheated is real. The marketplace Itch.io gave voice to the anti-NFT contingent in a tweet slamming the NFT craze, calling it a "scam," "get rich quick" scheme, and an avenue for dubious parties to exploit gamers. Security issues abound, such as the hacking of Axie Infinity's blockchain where hackers stole $625 million.

Gamers also decry the negative environmental impacts NFT minting and the blockchain inflict on the world. Ethereum, the main blockchain platform for NFTs, releases the same amount of carbon dioxide emissions into the atmosphere as the entire country of Libya. The enormous amount of energy consumption that occurs when minting, buying, and selling an NFT releases greenhouse gases that cause climate change. NFTs' carbon footprint is significant—the sale of one crypto art consumed 8.7 megawatt-hours of energy, the equivalent to two years' use of energy in an artist's studio.

NFTs Still the Future of Gaming?

Some gaming companies have acquiesced to the anti-NFT crowd and a few even agree with their view. Electronic Arts (EA), Team17, and Epic Games, have pumped the brakes on their NFT initiatives. Discord, STALKER 2, and MetaWorms canceled their NFT projects after being subject to backlash from gamers. Steam has banned all cryptocurrencies and NFTs from its online gaming platforms. Mojang's July 2022 announcement that it would ban NFTs from its wildly popular Minecraft game sent shockwaves through the gaming and NFT communities. Citing a desire to foster a safe and inclusive experience for its players, Minecraft has prohibited the integration of blockchain servers.

Despite several gaming companies abandoning, or at least taking a step back from NFTs, others continue to embrace them.

Perhaps they are banking on attracting the "silent majority" of gamers who are intrigued by the potential of earning NFTs from their activities. A survey of 1,500 players earlier this year revealed that only 23 percent were "not interested" or "not very interested" in play-to-earn NFTs. In fact, the poll revealed that more than two-thirds are already doing so, including 4 percent who are using video games to build their NFT collection and another 12 percent who have already monetized their play by selling NFTs they have earned. According to Interpret, the firm distributing the survey, "NFTs could play a major role in retention (of critical importance to live-service games), as over 45 percent indicated that being able to earn NFTs through gaming would increase their current engagement levels with games. Ultimately, Interpret expects gamer sentiment to continue to warm towards "play-to-earn" as the industry unpacks how best to position this new model. NFTs represent a shift in power to the players and provide a greater sense of true ownership from the items they earn both in and out-of-game."

Conclusion

Gaming companies will have to figure out the balance of using NFTs to enhance gaming experiences while compromising the experience for gamers who can't or refuse to utilize them. Due consideration of players' security and support needs as well as minimizing environmental impact will certainly help improve the outlook for NFT in gaming. Significantly, GameStop is moving ahead with its NFT marketplace. Others, like NFT World, which sold NFTs that fit into the Minecraft world, have committed to exploring other options, including developing a Minecraft competitor. But for now, a reckoning has arrived for the otherwise burgeoning crypto-based gaming market. While the gaming and NFT worlds are still evolving, game companies' romance with NFTs may have cooled for the foreseeable future.

Since the publication of this article in April 2022, Yuga Labs swiftly and expressly extended the same commercialization rights—including the creation of derivative works—that Bored Ape Yacht Club owners enjoy to Meebits and CryptoPunks owners. The confusion arose because the original CryptoPunks limited owners' rights to display their avatars; using them as business logos or otherwise leveraging them in any revenue-generating activity was prohibited. BAYC was one of the first NFT collections to transfer these rights, which normally are reserved for creators, under a decentralized collaboration license. The BAYC business model has been credited with driving higher prices for the original collection; all 10,000 apes have sold, generating an estimated market value of $1 billion.

Bored Apes Monkeying With Punks' Licenses?

On March 12, after weeks of online rumors and speculation, Yuga Labs, the company responsible for the Bored Ape Yacht Club (BAYC) and the Mutant Ape Yacht Club

(MAYC) NFT collections announced its acquisition of CryptoPunks and Meebits from the well-known mobile software company Larva Labs. BAYC, a popular collection of 10,000 unique bored NFT apes, has generated more than $1 billion in total sales amid celebrities flocking to the NFT bandwagon. After this acquisition, Yuga Labs now owns 423 CryptoPunks and 1,711 Meebits. In this article, we examine the details of the acquisition, what it means for emerging technologies companies, and specific issues related to intellectual property (IP) ownership and rights in NFTs.

IP Ownership

The acquisition shifts the IP ownership from Larva to Yuga; Yuga now owns the brand, the artworks, and other IP rights for both collections. As a result of the change in IP ownership, going forward CryptoPunks and Meebits holders will be granted the same commercial rights as BAYC owners. That means they will be able to commercialize their collectibles through a similar structure. Yuga Labs expects this development to increase the presence of the two collections on the metaverse and other related projects. Nonetheless, Yuga Labs acknowledges that Larva Labs' projects are historical collections with established communities. It has therefore not adopted the "club" model it used for BAYC.

IP License

There is some confusion about the rights CryptoPunk owners hold with regard to their avatars and the associated licenses. When Larva Labs launched the CryptoPunks NFTs, its website did not discuss licensing terms or provide a content license or permissible use of the artwork or characters. Even their terms and conditions did not include licensing stipulations or touch upon copyrights or commercial usage. In December 2021, several CryptoPunks NFT holders expressed their frustration with the lack of communication and guidance from Larva Labs concerning licensing and IP issues. NFT holders, minters, acquirers, and other stakeholders were left to ponder several questions:

- What was the scope of the license?
- Under what circumstances could the license be revoked or terminated?
- What was the validity of the DMCA provisions?
- To what extent could license terms be adopted by an NFT minter after NFTs have already been issued?
- What were the legal implications of product recalls in the NFT context?

The acquisition of CryptoPunks NFT by YugaLabs should help provide clarity on some of these issues.

Structure and Model

Historically, there is a stark difference between the way Yuga Labs and Larva Labs have managed IP rights. Larva Labs initially retained the IP rights to its creations, while Yuga Labs granted commercial rights to NFT owners. According to Yuga, the acquisition bestowed upon CryptoPunks and Meebits owners "the same commercial rights that BAYC and MAYC owners enjoy." The deal suggests that there are several ways to structure the sale of these NFTs. They can be sold on a standalone basis or combined with other offerings. An attorney experienced in digital technology, licensing, and transactions can provide valuable counsel for parties contemplating a similar transfer of assets.

DMCA Takedown Notices

The absence of clearly written legal terms and a bug in the purchase payment protocol prompted Larva Labs to issue a Digital Millennium Copyright Act (DMCA) takedown notice to the OpenSea NFT marketplace for the original CryptoPunks issue. OpenSea complied, delisting Version 1, which Larva had replaced with identical V2 avatars after correcting the bug. V1 CryptoPunks owners responded with a DMCA counter-notification challenging the legitimacy of the take-down notice and seeking reinstatement by OpenSea. V1 CryptoPunks was eventually reinstated, but it remains to be seen how Yuga will handle the issue moving forward. Will it allow CryptoPunk NFT owners to submit a counter-notification to an NFT marketplace in response to the minter's takedown or will there be some other mechanism in place?

Conclusion

The acquisition of Cryptopunks by Yuga Labs has exposed serious loopholes related to copyright ownership and licensing with regard to NFTs. It has highlighted the importance of having well-defined licensing terms, as the ultimate financial potential of an NFT lies within the scope of commercialization terms in the relevant grant of license. As a rule of thumb, licensing deals are likely to favor well-established brands over new and generative business models looking to cash in on the NFT gold rush. Incumbents and new entrants to the NFT space should be cautious before entering into any licensing deal related to NFTs and be sure to consult an attorney with current expertise in NFTs, intellectual property, licensing, and their broader legal implications.

ENTREPRENEURS, INDUSTRIES, AND BUSINESS MODELS

NFTs' foothold in the music industry continued to expand even as the value of NFTs as a whole bottomed out in mid-2022. Many artists exploited non-fungible tokens to support indie efforts as fan-based crowdfunding initiatives. The typical approach solicits cash that artists use to pay for a song or album's production and distribution. Donors receive shares of the creative product, and when revenues reach a certain level—often through streaming royalties—donors can cash in. Some musicians have awarded shares to people who provide services in association with a song's release. People involved in the NFT project can earn fractional royalty rights for everything from marketing and publicity to designing album covers, recruiting fan club members, and other missions.

NFTs Changing the Score In the Music Industry

Take note! Non-fungible Tokens (NFTs) have officially entered the music scene and are already moving beyond provable ownership of audio files: the latest development is NFTs that are created to be virtual celebrities. These NFTs

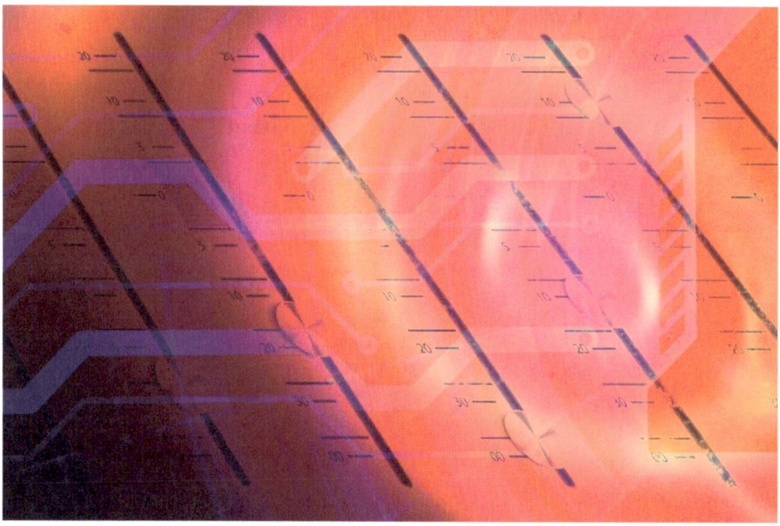

will even appear across multiple media types and platforms, including music videos and video games. Interest surrounding avatar-based NFTs is growing rapidly and even mega-celebrities are minting and investing in NFTs, from Paris Hilton to Jimmy Fallon to Steph Curry to Eminem (just don't ask Ye, aka Kanye West). Sales of NFTs are staggering, increasing from $95 million in 2020 to $25 billion in 2021.

NFT Avatars – America's Next Rockstars?

NFTs are being created based on songs, albums, music, lyrics, and soundbites and they are also being combined with music and digital art as .gifs and .jpgs to create unique, multimedia packages. Some NFTs even append PDFs to include additional content, such as lyrics or a message from the artist.

The band Kings of Leon released the first NFT-based music album in 2021. Well-known NFT creator Jace Kay created a virtual band called "The NFTs" and even created a song, "I've Got a Cool Cat Too" celebrating the popular Cool Cats collection of NFT felines. The NFTs plan to release their own music video along with the song as NFTs in the near future. The NFTs consist of four virtual band members, backed by real-life people: three sporting characters from the StereoheadZ NFT collection and a manager—none other than legendary Bored Ape Yacht Club's Captain Trippy. Their music is hosted on Spotify and Apple Music. The value of the NFTs value will be tied to the "celebrity's" popularity rather than the value of the token itself. As music NFTs become more popular, there are plans to collaborate with other artists through these tokens.

In order to purchase one of these music NFTs, potential buyers must be members of the StereoheadZ Music Club. Owners of these music NFTs receive full rights to create derivatives and use their characters in media, stories, and other digital platforms, and manage their social media. Additionally, the StereoheadZ will host a "Battle of the Bandz" competition to discover and promote music groups within their community. Their own music label, SZMC Music, will support the discovery, recording, management, and promotion of new bands.

Major music labels, studios, and promoters are getting involved as well. Earlier this year, Warner Music Group, which includes the iconic labels Atlantic and Warner Records and a number of famous musicians like Ed Sheeran, Lizzo, and Dua Lipa, announced that it will create exclusive NFTs for a range of artists in conjunction with OneOf, a "green" Web3 company, and Blockparty, a decentralized exchange (DEX) for NFTs. They are offering a range of NFTs from collectible and generative profile pics (PFPs) to music royalties and experiences. The collaboration is producing NFTs that will effectively live like real celebrities by earning income through music videos, animations, music shows, and even tickets for events such as Coachella. Moreover, these collaborations cut out middlemen so artists can connect directly with their fans and control their art mediums like never before.

Owners of NFTs can even send them to "auditions" for music videos and more. Jace Kay created the AvaCast platform to cast other NFTs, such as Bored Apes, Cool Cats, and StereoheadZ, in music videos. NFTs can have their own music careers, whether it is recording songs or making music videos. Of course, the NFTs will be managed by their owners. Warner Music Group will announce its own "casting calls" for NFTs.

Music NFTs can also be used to raise money for charitable causes. NFTs can even be designed to sell existing works of music, whether for profit or for charity. The StereoheadZ

Music Community will donate a portion of the NFT sales towards the SZMC Community Fund, which will help foster the creativity and collaboration of the club's members.

Late last year, a previously unreleased Whitney Houston recording she made when she was 17 was minted as an NFT. Placed on the OneOf NFT auction platform, it sold for $1 million, the highest-priced NFT on the Tezos (XTZ) blockchain. While the new NFT owner can access the full version of the song, the NFT contract did not include rights to the recording itself or to publish it elsewhere to reveal the song. Proceeds from the sale went to the Whitney E. Houston Legacy Foundation which supports other budding music artists.

Music NFTs and Smart Contracts—Legal Issues

While music NFTs provide enormous potential for artists to control their own works and careers, there are legal issues to be considered. In the past, it was not unusual for artists to receive compensation for their work but forfeit the rights to their intellectual property. Further benefits of utilizing NFTs in music are that artists can receive ongoing and accurate royalty payments for their work and also have more say over the content of their music. Blockchain and NFTs readily enable primary and secondary resell rights, so artists can create contracts that both record and execute their right to receive royalties for the future use and resale of their works. Whereas previously music studios would typically control what an artist could do and largely dictate how much they would make in their contracts, NFTs allow artists far greater control over their intellectual property and royalty structures.

Since each NFT is unique, the smart contract is recorded on the blockchain with the terms the artists want, without having to negotiate with other parties. Additionally, these smart contracts can account for equity crowdfunding initiatives, so each contributor can be included in whatever compensation scheme is appropriate, such as a percentage of revenues or lifetime tickets. NFTs enable smart contracts to be written so artists are directly compensated, and any crowdfund contributors get their fair share when music NFTs are bought and sold.

Furthermore, music NFTs can be configured in their smart contacts to be "upgradeable," which means they are non-static digital assets. An upgradeable NFT will respond to some event or trigger that occurs either on or off a blockchain, such as a ticket sale for a concert going ahead. This also enables original creators and future collaborators to all receive credit or permission to transform the content. Typically, making a remix of an already published song would involve first obtaining permission from the original artist and any other copyright holders to avoid copyright violations and/or obtaining a license for performance rights. With an upgradeable NFT, the original creator maintains these intellectual property rights but can provide for downstream owners of the NFT to remix the content and make it their own derivative works.

Music NFTs have the potential to transform the industry, giving artists greater control over their works, ensuring they receive accurate and higher compensation, raising money for good causes, cutting out middle people, and enhancing the consumer experience through closer one-to-one contact between artists and fans. The possibilities are endless. Thanks to blockchain and smart contracts, NFTs can enable artists and creators to take greater control over their destinities than ever before.

Quentin Tarantino and Miramax settled their lawsuit in September 2022. Though terms were not disclosed, the parties issued a joint statement that they would be asking the court to drop the case. Apparently, there are no hard feelings. According to the statement "the parties have agreed to put this matter behind them and look forward to collaborating with each other on future projects, including possible NFTs."

Lights! Camera! Token!
Are NFTs Ready for Their Big Closeup?

Non-fungible tokens (NFTs) are once again proving their versatility. Entrepreneurs have found a variety of compelling uses for them in video games, drink recipes, digital art, fantasy sports, and more. Now, the movie industry is joining the picture by launching its own NFTs. Creating NFTs for films has been gaining steam, whether for enhancing the real-time theater experience, selling merchandise, raising capital for independent films, promoting new releases, or generating nostalgia for classic cinema.

The Film Industry Looks to NFTs for New Experiences

With the waning of COVID-19 and the reopening of entertainment venues, movie studios are looking for new ways to enhance fans' viewing experience. Way back in 2018, 20th Century Fox used limited edition digital poster NFTs to promote *Deadpool 2*. For the release of *Godzilla vs. Kong*, Legendary Entertainment announced it would issue a specially-created NFT collection on the movie's release date, marking the first NFT collection by a major studio. The NFTs were created by Australian digital concept artist BossLogic (Kode Abdo) and secured by digital blockchain technology.

In 2021, the *Matrix* universe announced its own NFT collection, but instead of digital art, these NFTs would comprise human avatars. Produced in collaboration with the Nifty's marketplace, these NFTs were built using Epic Games' MetaHuman Creator and went on sale on November 30. Each human avatar is randomly generated, and users could insert themselves into the Matrix universe as unique characters. The avatars were so popular that the vendor's website crashed within moments of launch. Once the glitch was corrected, all 100,000 avatars sold out in less than a week. Buyers of the Matrix NFTs do not own the commercial rights to the avatars. NFT creators, however, should be aware of a film's copyright status and other contractual issues covering film copyrights, trademarks, publicity rights, and other legal issues.

A Brief Primer on Copyright Law

Under Article I, Section 8, Clause 8 of the US Constitution, copyrights expire after a certain amount of time—they cannot go on forever – in order to promote the progress of science and useful arts for the public. Until their copyrights expire, however, copyright creators maintain the exclusive right to use and profit from their creations and discoveries. This clause forms the basis of intellectual property laws in the US.

Copyrights protect original works of authorship fixed in a tangible medium, whether they are published or unpublished. Housed in Title 17 of the U.S. Code, the Copyright Act of 1976 provided a comprehensive revision of the law, recognizing fair use and specifying that copyright extends to a creator's expression or interpretation of concepts but not to the ideas and procedures themselves. Unfortunately, there is no comprehensive list of films in the public domain, but some books and websites (including Wikipedia) have tried to keep track of films that have moved into the public domain.

Generally, copyright expiration rules differ depending on when the protections were instantiated. Original works of authorship, including movies, made prior to 1978, are protected for a maximum of 95 years from the date of publication, subject to renewal during the 28th year following publication. For movies made or copyrighted in 1978 or later, protections will expire, and the movie will move into the public domain, 70 years after the creator's death. Most movies made before 1926 are now in the public domain. However, NFT creators, in particular, must be careful when using movie clips to avoid running afoul of copyright holders.

Copyright Issues with Historical Film Rights

For NFT collectors who love cult classics and films from the Golden Age of cinema, Quentin Tarantino's "Pulp Fiction" NFT series which is soon to be launched on OpenSea, will depict scenes from the film in addition to the release of "secrets" that include never-before-seen footage, outtakes, uncut original handwritten scripts, and director's commentary. Collectors can keep the secrets to themselves, share with a few friends, or disclose them to the world. These "Secret NFTs" represent a new asset class that lives on the Secret Network. Designed after the Ethereum blockchain, they have programmable privacy features, an optional private metadata field, support private ownership, and allow creators to determine access control.

NFTs can offer filmmakers additional income streams. But they must own the film – and soundtrack – rights to use movie clips for NFTs. Tarantino is finding this out, as he has already been sued by Miramax which is seeking to halt his sale of *Pulp Fiction* NFTs. The lawsuit alleges that Tarantino's contractual film rights extend only to interactive games, live performances, and other ancillary media, and do not include NFTs. Additionally, the lawsuit claims that while Tarantino can "publish" pieces of his screenplay, his rights do not extend to NFTs.

Who Owns the Rights to These Films?

Filmmaking is perhaps one of the most convoluted exercises in terms of intellectual property rights. So many people can be involved in each stage of the movie-making process, from script to screen and even post-release with the rise of NFTs.

Generally, film copyright belongs to the person or entity who arranged for the film to be made. The production house/producer of the film usually possesses the rights to the movie, but individual investors may also hold the copyright. The copyright holder will only own the moving images and sounds of the film but not necessarily the underlying works in the film such as the music or the script. However, copyrights to films can also be determined by a contractual agreement, which can divide the copyrights in a number of ways, such as over a certain period of time, through employment contracts, literary rights, as well as for creating derivative works like NFTs that use the film content. All transfer of copyrights must be in writing and the chain of title unbroken.

So far, these rules apply to NFTs as well. As the lawsuit between Tarantino and Miramax demonstrates, the legality of NFTs and film copyrights are still a bit fuzzy in this case because the contract was executed before NFTs existed. Yet, NFT owners should be aware that an NFT purchase does not mean that they own any rights to the film themselves—only the NFT itself. Creators of NFTs should be aware of copyright laws to determine who owns the copyrights to a certain film.

Indie Filmmakers Using NFTs to Attract Angels

Another interesting development on NFTs and movie rights is that independent filmmakers are also getting into the game. Directors, producers, distributors, and financiers are always looking for the next box office smash in independent cinema. In April 2021, Kevin Smith (of Jay and Silent Bob fame) announced he would auction an NFT for his indie film *Killroy Was Here*. Instead of selling the movie directly to a studio (like he did for *Clerks*), Smith is selling the film itself – complete with distribution rights – as an NFT.

Director Jennifer Esposito is using a unique combination of an NFT auction and a public offering to sell shares in her next independent film. After the film's release, shareholders will receive a portion of the revenues and the shares will convert to copyrights. Independent filmmakers are exploring NFTs as a means to finance projects and bypass traditional Hollywood funding as well as copyrights.

Another filmmaker, Niels Juul, who is known for his work with Martin Scorsese, is seeking to finance his own Hollywood production entirely by auctioning NFTs. As the founder of NFT Studios, his model aims to bypass the traditional Hollywood funding mechanisms to bring films to the screen faster and so disrupt the trend for independent films to take quite a while to find buyers and be distributed by studios. A mix of NFT investment entities and private buyers, these films will have multiple owners who will get a cut of the profits and licensing rights among other related benefits.

NFTs have already begun to prove their worth. The Hollywood-meets-NFT scene is booming. However, the latest copyright laws do not consider NFTs and film rights because they are a recent development. While Hollywood studios are cashing in on the NFTs, movie directors and writers will need to take measures in future movie contracts to account for their NFT rights.

The Role of Law Enforcement in Detecting, Investigating, and Prosecuting Criminal Activity Related to Digital Assets, *a report prepared by the Department of Justice's National Cryptocurrency Enforcement Team ("NCET") in consultation with the Treasury and Homeland Security departments and multiple federal regulatory agencies included a suggestion that the 1970 Bank Secrecy Act be amended to expressly state that its key AML provisions apply to NFT platforms, including online auction houses and digital art galleries. The report is part of the Biden administration's digital asset framework, a set of recommendations and guidelines for regulating not only NFTs but also cryptocurrencies, transactions, and fraud prevention.*

Defining NFTs: Property, Securities, or Commodities?

The legal classification and regulatory environment for NFTs remain unclear, making it difficult for Web3 developers, video game publishers, and metaverse architects to be fully confident they can employ NFTs without inviting lawsuits or government investigations. Some semblances of clarity,

however, may be on the horizon, as US courts in the near future will decide several potential landmark cases, regulators deliver commentary that hints at pending rulings, and industry groups weigh in with suggestions for self-policing.

Securities, Commodities, or Property?

Defining NFTs' status among personal and business assets is a logical first step in determining whether and how they should be regulated. Some experts are convinced that NFTs constitute securities because they act as investment instruments. People purchase them in the hope that their uniqueness and scarcity will drive up their value so they can be sold at a profit.

Several high-profile court cases hinge on plaintiffs' contention that NFTs are securities. The US Department of Justice has accused Nate Chastain, a former OpenSea executive, of insider trading based on confidential information about upcoming issuances that OpenSea would promote. The government alleges that he purchased many of those NFTs in advance and profited when the ensuing publicity on the platform increased demand and drove prices higher. Chastain's attorneys argue that even if Chastain did as the DOJ alleges, he should not be prosecuted because his actions would not constitute criminal activity. Insider trading, they say, is only illegal if it is done using stocks or other securities and NFTs are not securities. In this view, Chastain's actions may be the definition of workplace misconduct, but they do not rise to the level of a federal felony.

Many business models adopted by video game and Web3 companies leverage the collectability of NFTs. That's the premise behind NBA Top Shots Moments. The National Basketball Association contracted with Dapper Labs to distribute the Moments, which are video clips from NBA games. The value of Moments with low serial numbers, featuring stars of the game, and capturing stellar plays consistently rises to well above their initial selling price. A class action lawsuit alleges that Dapper Labs violates US securities law by actively promoting, offering, and selling the NFTs. Plaintiffs argue that Dapper Labs failed to comply with the securities disclosure requirements, downplaying the investment risks involved and inducing uninformed purchases. Dapper Labs counters that Moments are not investments, but rather simply digital basketball cards offered to fans and collectors.

Finally, a Senate bill would classify most NFTs as commodities and weaken the Securities and Exchange Commission's oversight powers. The bulk of regulatory duties instead would fall to the Commodity Futures Trading Commission, whose mission is to protect buyers, sellers, and the public from fraud, investigate misconduct and minimize the risks inherent in derivatives transactions. Categorizing NFTs as commodities would impose strict disclosure requirements, trading guidelines, and marketing standards upon sellers. Companies that allow buyers to obtain NFTs on margin or through leveraged accounts would have to operate on registered exchanges or make physical delivery of the NFT and/or the asset tied to it within four weeks of purchase.

The outcome of these court cases and the fate of the Senate bill will further define how NFTs are regulated, taxed, and transacted.

AML/KYC

According to a report issued by Elliptic, a London-based blockchain analysis company, over $540 million in crypto proceeds were processed through money laundering schemes over the last two years, including over $153 million that allegedly originated from ransomware payments. The study found that 22 NFT marketplaces, 4 NFT-based games or metaverse platforms, and 2 NFT swap services were being investigated for money laundering.

In February 2022, the United States Department of the Treasury issued a *Study of the Facilitation of Money Laundering and Terror Finance Through the Trade in Works of Art*. The report discusses how the high-value art market, including certain NFTs, is vulnerable to financial crime and susceptible to abuse by bad actors. It also makes recommendations for art market participants to implement and maintain anti-money laundering/countering financing of terrorism (AML/CFT) programs. Similarly, in April 2022, a consortium of governing bodies, including the Internal Revenue Service, issued warnings to banks, legal authorities, and private collectors about the growing money laundering and fraud risks surrounding NFTs. This consortium is known as the Joint Chiefs of Global Tax Enforcement and was formed in 2018 to share intelligence and combat transnational tax crimes. Given these developments, it is likely that the US will require KYC measures to fight money laundering related to NFTs in the near future.

Intellectual Property

It is well established that buying an NFT does not grant ownership over the underlying asset unless that transfer is expressly stated in the smart contract that enables the transaction. In fact, according to a recent study conducted by crypto merchant bank Galaxy Digital on the NFT marketplace, Web3's promise of digital ownership and property rights "remains far off." The study found that the vast majority of top NFT collections do not convey any form of intellectual property or ownership of underlying artwork or media. Nonetheless, this has not prevented many NFT buyers and sellers from trying to convince themselves and others that owning a screenplay, a handbag, a shoe, or some other possession grants them the right to mint digital assets based on them.

For example, Miramax sued to prohibit Quentin Tarantino from selling NFTs based on *Pulp Fiction*. The studio's recently settled suit noted that simply having written the screenplay does not convey IP rights to Tarantino to the movie. Tarantino's view was that the NFTs were derivative of the screenplay, not the production.

Several other cases pertaining to NFTs and IP loom. Courts will decide a host of thorny NFT issues related to trademark infringement, copyright, and right of publicity. The recent spate of litigation pertaining to NFTs and IP suggests that new regulations may be required to address how innovators are employing NFTs in gaming and virtual worlds.

Privacy

The blockchain on which NFTs are based is a public ledger, which means that anyone in the world can view its contents. The blockchain is also immutable: information contained within it cannot be altered or deleted. These factors give rise to significant privacy and data protection concerns related to NFTs. Hackers could potentially use NFT transactions to steal users' blockchain addresses, financial activity, physical location, metaverse avatars, and more.

Given the dynamic and relatively young state of gaming, metaverse, and other digital technologies, there are no laws that specifically tackle privacy and data protection over the blockchain. Current data protection laws in the US and other countries are inadequate to address privacy-related challenges posed by the increasing use of NFTs. For example, the fact that data cannot be deleted from the blockchain runs contrary to basic data subject rights under the California Consumer

Privacy Act. It seems likely that the US will eventually introduce new laws to reconcile these disconnects.

Conclusion

As an emerging asset class, NFTs and their marketplaces require a new set of guidelines and rules for consumer protection, particularly with regard to NFTs' classification, IP ownership, and security.

In order to avoid or minimize legal risk, game publishers, metaverse developers, and web entrepreneurs should protect themselves by speaking with an attorney before embarking on any NFT project.

Since the publication of this article in the Fall of 2021, innovative sports NFT companies have taken the ball and run with it. For instance, PolySports not only incorporates collectible, tradable NFTs but imbues them with powers and value within its platform. Players who purchase or earn NFTs through gameplay can leverage them to enter tournaments and competitions for free and accelerate the rewards they earn. PolySports and Sorare are just two companies working to infuse NFTs with utilitarian value within their platform. This approach may breathe new life into NFT ownership, extending its appeal beyond the investment community.

NFTs Transform the Multibillion-dollar Fantasy Sports Industry

Non-fungible tokens (NFTs) are making headlines again, this time in fantasy sports. In September 2021, the French start-up company Sorare announced that it had raised significant capital—$680 million to be exact—for its fantasy football (soccer) platform. What makes this new format unique is the use of non-fungible tokens (NFTs) in conjunction with

fantasy sports and blockchain technology to track transactions within the fantasy league. While there may be some skepticism around NFTs, fantasy sports companies seem primed to survive and grow.

Fantasy Sports Still Reign Supreme

Fantasy sports are online gaming platforms that enable a participant to draft, sign, manage, and trade professional athletes to build their own teams and compete against other teams "owners," either head-to-head in weekly leagues or season-long "Rotisserie-style" scoring. Points are awarded based on the players' actual performance in their real-life games. In 2019, fantasy sports generated $2.9 billion and the sector was valued at approximately $7.22 billion. The industry shows little sign of slowing down, especially now with the introduction of NFTs to the mix. According to Research and Markets, the global fantasy sports market is expected to have a CAGR of 5 percent from 2020 to 2025. Opportunities for fantasy sports leagues to grow are myriad, especially as internet access and 5G networks continue to proliferate. Allied Market Research predicts that fantasy sports will reach $48.6 billion by 2027, a CAGR of 13.9 percent from 2021 to 2027.

The Ever-Expanding Role of NFTs in Fantasy Sports

In 2021, NFTs have taken an all-star role in fantasy sports, with companies making millions by issuing new cards on their platforms. These companies use blockchain technology distributed across thousands of computers around the world to record who owns which "cards" and ensure that all purchases and sales are accurate and transparent.

- ***Sorare***—This company in particular has created a unique approach to its NFTs and fantasy football platform. The company has built a fantasy sports league centered on buying, collecting, and trading NFTs on the Ethereum blockchain. The company partnered with 180 football organizations, including the European giants Real Madrid, Liverpool, and Juventus. Even current and former top European players have invested in the company, with Gerard Pique, Antione Griezmann, and Rio Ferdinand taking stakes. Since January 2021, over $150 million worth of NFTs has been traded on their platform with sales growing fifty-fold between Q2 2020 and Q2 2021. Valued currently at $4.3 billion, the card company boasts 600,000 registered users, including 150,000 who buy, sell, or trade cards every month. Sorare generates revenue by issuing new cards on its platform through auctions. Cards can also be sold on platforms such as OpenSea and Rarible.

- ***NBA TopShot***—Since opening its doors in October 2020, NBA Top Shot has generated $500 million in sales of basketball themed NFTs and attracted over 800,000 users. Dapper Labs, the developer of NBA Top Shots, is now worth $2.6 billion and boasts a line-up of famous investors that includes Hollywood stars, current NBA players, and Michael Jordan. Like other platforms, participants can buy, sell, and trade officially licensed video highlights of their favorite players. Purchasers don't receive the copyright to the image—they get ownership over the NFT only. Pursuant to an agreement with the NBA and Dapper Labs, the NFT cannot be divided or copied by the purchaser and only transactions expressly outlined in the contract are allowed. Top Shot recently sold a LeBron James highlight NFT for over $200,000.

- ***Ultimate NFT***—The recently formed Ultimate NFT goes one step further. It has developed a fantasy sports platform that adds a play-to-earn system to NFTs and fantasy football. Players use their NFTs to build fantasy dynasties and collect points based on the performance of the real-life players represented in their games. Ultimate NFT uses smart contracts to ensure players can earn money without intervention from "centralized powers" and enables borderless transactions. Their content aims to launch in mid/late October 2021.

Legal issues relating to NFTs, Fantasy Sports, and Leagues

- ***Blockchain, traceability, and smart contracts***—As discussed in a previous Gamma Law blog, the blockchain is vital for tracing and tracking NFTs through smart contracts, which are stored on the blockchain. They can be used in conjunction with traditional contracts to enforce rights in connection with NFTs. Smart contracts are specific, irrevocable, automatically executing contracts that exist on the blockchain platform.

  Transactions are transparent, traceable, and cannot be reversed. With NFTs specifically, Ethereum is the dominant smart contract network and smart contracts are executed on the Ethereum Virtual Machine (EVM). These online, smart contracts may be enforceable under the Uniform Commercial Code – in particular, pursuant to Article 9 – as well as under contract law. Smart contracts can improve accountability in any type of binding agreement by automating the formation and enforcement of promises. At their core, they are designed to prevent cheating—whether by undermining the card creator's IP rights, illegally entering a card on the platform, or copying a player's NFT.

- ***Licensing rights***—NFTs have changed the legal landscape surrounding image licensing for sports.

When a piece of art or music or a sports personality is involved in an NFT, licensing rights come into play.

Contracts with NFT sports cards may include provisions to protect the rights of the player, the purchaser, the creator, and the platform, and in some situations, this may lead to a variety of conditions surrounding the subsequent use of the NFT:

- Transferring permissions to a third-party
- Whether or how the creator or the player will be compensated
- How the NFT can be used by the purchaser, such as for commercial usage
- Whether the NFT owner can copy and sell the card, and if so, how the revenues would be split between the owner, creator, and player
- Whether the NFT owner can create derivatives or modifications from the card and if so, how they can use them.

The relevant sports league and NFT fantasy sports companies enter licensing agreements that determine the rights that are transferred with the NFTs, so any purchaser of the NFTs should fully read and understand the scope of their rights before considering actions such as copying or dividing NFTs into parts.

- ***Name, Image, Likeness Rights***— NFTs present another opportunity for professional and college athletes to profit from their names, images, or likenesses (NIL), also known as the right of publicity as well as through trademarks, copyrights, and contract law. Individual professional athletes may negotiate image rights with NFT companies or individual NFT creators. Usually, a player's contract will determine which image rights they retain, what the league owns, and what they are free to negotiate with other companies. Notably, while a player will hold the rights to his or her image in certain jurisdictions, US courts have held that the First Amendment may allow fantasy sports teams to use athletes' likenesses, names, statistics, and other newsworthy content without licensing or compensation.

Additionally, if an NFT contains a video or photo of a sporting event, the purchaser might become entangled in the legal issue of who actually owns the content—the league, the player, or the creator. Like so much in the legal realm, it depends! Sports photographers may hold exclusive rights to the photos they take during a game. Professional athletes may use personal photos that were in their possession to create NFTs. Or, the NFT company, the league, and the player's union can negotiate rights in NFTs licensing agreements discussed previously, such as the NBA, Dapper Labs, and the NBA Player Association did for NBA TopShop.

- ***Gambling***—Participants and investors in NFT-based fantasy leagues should also be aware of the gambling laws in their jurisdictions. The legality of fantasy sports leagues is often tied to gambling laws and laws pertaining to games of skill. Fantasy sports are often conflated with online sports gambling, and the latter can be illegal in certain jurisdictions. While the Unlawful Internet Gambling Enforcement Act of 2006 prohibits online gambling to protect consumers, it specifically excludes fantasy sports leagues because they are considered skills-based games rather than games of chance. However, state laws take differing approaches to regulating fantasy sports. Participants in a fantasy league can bet on fantasy sports games (if legal in their state), but not on actual real-life games. Sports gambling in the US still remains highly regulated and controlled, so fantasy sports participants should be aware of any platforms that offer gambling options.

NFTs and fantasy sports have tremendous potential to expand with the support of major leagues, sports clubs, players' associations, and consumers who want to enter the NFT market. However, in order for the NFT collectors to have the best experience possible, it is important for these possible legal snags to be ironed out before thousands of new and potentially unsuspecting participants enter the market.

A Morning Consult *survey found that 58 percent of Esports enthusiasts are interested in the NFT market, easily making them the most optimistic demographic. The vicarious thrill sports fans receive when their teams win and the desire to be a part of that success is driving the popularity of Esports NFTs. Fan tokens bring Esports fans closer to the action. Some of these tokens entitle owners to attend exclusive events and interact with players. A growing trend sees Esports teams allowing NFT owners to have a say in strategies, club management, and other operational decisions.*

Leveling the Playing Field: Regulation of Esports NFTs

Many believe that non-fungible tokens (NFTs) are poised to revolutionize the esports industry. Current applications of NFTs in esports include awarding NFTs in place of physical tournament trophies, which is a much more efficient solution given the prevalence of online competitions today; and game publishers and esports organizations such as 100 Thieves and Simplicity Esports are integrating NFTs into consumer

offerings in the form of digital player cards and collectible trading cards. While these applications represent just the start of what may become a booming use of NFTs in esports, currently there is little information available on related legal and regulatory issues. This article examines some important legal considerations related to the use of NFTs in this exciting environment.

Scope of Rights

An NFT typically represents a type of license attached to a specific digital asset—an image, sound bite or video clip, etc. In most cases, the copyright to the underlying art or other asset is retained by the owner of the physical asset. It is important to understand that buying an NFT does not automatically give the purchaser the rights to the digital media file itself. Only the token changes hands, so companies seeking to memorialize esports highlights as NFTs should obtain the rights to the events from the rights holders unless the fair-use doctrine or other exception applies.

Licensing Issues

In the case of esports NFTs, intellectual property (IP) licensing can become complicated, as several entities could claim a stake in a transaction. This includes but is not limited to players, teams, leagues, game publishers, and tournament promoters. Creators of esports-based NFTs should protect themselves by obtaining the proper license for any intellectual or creative property they do not own. NFTs that incorporate (or simply appropriate) third-party IP without permission set themselves up for a lawsuit. Contracts for esports NFT licensing rights should cover three broad areas:

1. **Scope and Limitations**—Both the licensee and the licensor should be clear about what rights are granted in a sale and even whether those rights can legally be transferred. Sellers will want to limit what the buyer

can do with the NFT while the buyer will want to obtain as much leeway as possible for the licensing fee. The permissions being transferred should be expressly stated in the contract. Generally, the license will reserve all other rights for the IP owner—not the NFT owner. For example, to maintain scarcity and value, a creator may grant another party the right to create a limited number of NFTs associated with a copyrighted work. Further, a licensor may choose to expressly prohibit, or impose restrictions on the licensee to create NFTs based on modifications of the underlying work. This is particularly important given the growing trend of layered, programmable, and generative art.

2. **Content Restrictions**—The murky and sometimes clandestine world of NFT creation has led some minters, either through ignorance or malfeasance, to incorporate third-party IP without permission. IP owners have taken note and begun protecting their creative output through vigilance and enforcement efforts. Game publishers and esports companies must adhere to content restrictions related to the use of third-party IP. It is also important to have the necessary prior permission in order to avoid legal liability.

3. **Revenue Split**—Game publishers and esports participants should clearly delineate how any revenues generated as a result of an NFT arrangement will be allocated. Revenue split or profit-sharing provisions in the license agreement are critical because many IP owners grant rights to create NFTs based on their IP with the intention of getting paid, not only on the initial sale of the NFTs but on subsequent sales as well via smart contracts.

Name, Image, and Likeness (NIL)—As highlighted by NCAA athletes' recent win regarding their right to profit from their names, images, and likenesses, esports companies must understand their responsibilities with regard to NIL. As of this year, collegiate athletes in many states now can earn money and/or merchandise for appearing in advertisements, making endorsements, or otherwise promoting products and services. Game publishers and esports companies should be mindful of these developments to be aware of the appropriate licensing requirements, prepare comprehensive contracts, and distribute remuneration as and where necessary.

IP Protection

As game publishers and esports companies increasingly create their own tokenized assets, they should consider their own IP protection strategy. Brand owners may wish to extend their trademark registrations to cover the use and classification of NFTs. They may also choose to associate certain designs or trade dress (product packaging, labeling, layout, color, etc.) with their brand. Design patents may also be particularly valuable since profits from the sale and resale of NFTs can be significant. Unlike copyright protection or trademark protection, a design patent entitles the owner to the entirety of profits an infringer collects—not just the portion of profits attributable to the unauthorized use of the design. Appropriate legal mechanisms should be put in place to assure IP protection in tokenized assets and other digital collectibles.

Securities and Taxes

Teams selling esports fan tokens in the US may be walking a fine line between merchandising and securities dealing. As such, they must ensure that they comply with all these laws and securities-related regulations in particular. NFTs bought and sold on secondary markets must be structured such that the SEC does not view them as securities. If regulators deem an esports NFT to be an investment (rather than a collectible or an artistic bauble), they may seek to regulate it as a security.

Safeguards—Game publishers and esports companies are advised to implement robust terms and conditions, privacy policies, end-user agreements, copyright protection, and disclaimers to ensure their rights and shield themselves from legal action. This will also offer protection in the case of an allegation of direct or indirect infringement. An attorney specializing in esports and NFTs can help in drafting these legal documents.

It seems inevitable that NFTs will become increasingly prevalent in the booming esports market. In fact, there are already several examples of esports-based NFTs that surpassed $100 million in sales within a couple of months of launch. With so much money at stake, legal considerations related to the use of NFTs in esports such as the above are likely to become more pronounced. Due to the relatively nascent nature of NFTs, the regulatory landscape is still evolving. It is important to consult an attorney specializing in esports and NFTs before launching your own NFT. Nuanced legal advice at the inception of the NFT project can save you time, money, and resources down the road.

The liquor industry is one of the first to connect NFTs to physical assets encompassing tangible benefits. Just two months after this article was published in August 2021, BlockBar launched the world's first direct-to-consumer NFT marketplace. The company sells NFTs directly tied to bottles of rare and collectible bottles of wine and spirits. NFT purchasers can exchange their tokens for the bottles at any time. The company takes care of storing owners' bottles until they wish to take possession to display or—God forbid—actually drink them. Redeeming an NFT and assuming physical possession of a bottle removes it and the NFT from the marketplace, increasing the value of those still in circulation.

Hold My Beer: NFTs, Alcohol, and Intellectual Property

Lucrative non-fungible token (NFT) auction sales continue to generate headlines around the world. NFTs are unduplicable assets that are developed via blockchain technology and can be used to track their creators, their transactions, and their

owners. Sales of NFTs are typically conducted using ether, the cryptocurrency developed for the Ethereum blockchain.

Cryptocurrencies' value can be highly volatile and significantly affect the price and value of purchased NFTs. Most NFT merchants also list their prices in U.S. dollars. NFTs have sold for astronomical amounts: Jack Dorsey's first tweet went for over $2.9 million, a Beeple piece fetched $69 million at Christie's, and Crypto Punk's CovidAlien garnered $11.7 million at Sotheby's. NFT auctions are gaining in frequency and popularity, and more mainstream companies are entering the fray. NFTs up for auction range from NBA-certified basketballs to Coca-Cola's series of four NFTs designed by Tafi and depicting pixelated versions of Coke's classic 1956 vending machine.

Using Alcohol-based NFTs for Good Causes

Numerous NFTs are auctioned for the purpose of raising money for charities and good causes. With the COVID-19 pandemic shutting down many bars and restaurants, those working in the service and hospitality industries had to get creative. Even producers of alcoholic beverages are using NFTs to raise money for charitable causes. Stella Artois has released NFTs for auction to support the hospitality industry in the United Kingdom. One hundred percent of the original sale and 10 percent of each subsequent sale will be notated to the Stella Artois Tips campaign.

Bacardi announced on National Rum Day that it will hold an NFT auction on September 1, 2021, to raise funds for Black-owned bars. The NFT will showcase the release of its limited-edition rum Reserva Ocho Sherry Cask Finish. Bacardi will donate the proceeds to "Backing the B.A.R.," an initiative it co-sponsors with the NAACP to support African American-owned businesses.

Beer Companies Hop on the NFT Train

NFTs are brewing something of a happy hour among beer, wine, and alcohol companies. The microbrewery world is expanding into the NFT realm as part of its marketing efforts. Denver Beer Co auctioned a "Beer for Life" NFT, a one-of-a-kind NFT housed on the OpenSea platform.

The NFT comprises a unique spinning digital gold coin with the words "Beer For Life" on one side and the Denver Beer Co. logo on the other. The winner of the auction is entitled to up to four free beers per day for life at any Denver Beer Co taproom. The two-week auction closed on July 7, 2021, and the NFT sold for 4.33 ether or about $9,200 at the time of purchase. The owner can hang onto the NFT and use it to quench their thirst daily or sell it to someone else—the NFT itself is transferable and will not expire. Breweries are also selling NFTs to match real-life beers. Whistle Buoy Brewing Company announced in May 2021 that it was designing an NFT in conjunction with a special edition beer. It partnered with a local artist to create the limited-edition NFT which features a hand-numbered 32-ounce gold can. The brewery created an actual "NFT beer" that was available on draft and listed the NFT on OpenSea, where it sold for 0.22 ether, which is about $625.

Hard Liquor Also Takes Its Shot

Beer companies aren't the only ones dipping into NFTs. Cocktail-themed NFTs are getting into the mix and are selling for tidy sums. In April 2021, Quality-Eats sold a cocktail NFT, called Into the Ether, for 0.75 ether, or approximately $2,400. The company donated the NFT to ROAR NY to support restaurant workers impacted by COVID-19. Potential buyers browsing on the OpenSea NFT buying/selling platform can search through a catalog of cocktail NFTs. A recent sampling: the Tokyo Iced Tea Cocktail NFT was listed but had no price advertised; the Vodka Watermelon Cocktail

NFT was offered for 0.1 ether, which is about $320; “SunshineMint” was selling The Four Horsemen NFT for 0.5 ether, approximately $1,600.

A bartender or anyone else can “mint” a julep or any other cocktail recipe into an NFT that would digitally represent the cocktail. Once someone mints their recipe as an NFT, it basically acts as proof of copyright. The NFT cocktail recipe will reside on the blockchain indefinitely and the technology ensures it is always traceable to its creator. Bartenders even have created Instagram pages to advertise their cocktail NFT creations. Even though they sell the digital representation of their NFT through auction, creators, like all NFT minters, can negotiate how new owners are permitted to use and display the drink recipe.

Cocktail NFTs and Intellectual Property Considerations

Copyright laws usually do not protect recipes because they are considered “facts.” While drink makers are able to trademark the names of their beverages, there really isn’t much a bartender or mixologist can do. However, in the very near future, inventors of cocktails might use NFTs to claim ownership over their recipes.

That said, when an employee creates a cocktail recipe while on the clock, the intellectual property is commonly deemed to be a ”work product” and the property of their employer, a contractual arrangement exists stating otherwise. While contractors are able to keep rights to the drinks they make, they should still be actively aware of the potential for someone else to hijack their intellectual property. Bartenders might obtain copyright protection for cocktail recipes that qualify as “substantial literary expressions" and are in a tangible form. If a drink recipe is actually copyrighted, NFT creators would have no right to create an NFT based on it.

NFTs are one potential tool bartenders can use to retain intellectual property rights to a drink name or recipe that they have created. Under trademark law, a period of "excused non-use," allows a bar to temporarily discontinue offering a drink without immediately losing the rights to the cocktail's name. Drink names—rather than their recipes—are usually the subject of trademark registration. Yet, drink makers with a trademark must not fall into the trap of knowingly allowing or actively consenting to someone else acting in conflict with their trademark rights. In the past, many large alcohol companies have sued bars for using their brand name or signature drink name, as was the case with Pusser's Painkiller and Gosling's Dark and Stormy.

Creators of alcohol-based NFTs should consider any trade secret implications their drinks may stir up. They might fall foul of a "brand" cocktail situation in which the drink has a trademarked name, or the recipe is considered proprietary. Also, bars can protect themselves with bartender contracts that contain non-compete clauses that preclude employees from using the drink recipes created on the premises as the basis for NFTs.

Drink makers might also consider applying for patents for beverage recipes, but this process is lengthy and expensive. Despite this, the use of NFTs and patents are accelerating in the alcohol industry and elsewhere. Retailers are looking to patents to generate cryptographic digital assets for their goods, which would prove to a buyer that the goods are authentic – Nike has one such system. A patent application would require the minting bartender to disclose the drink recipe as part of the patent's transparency provision. A person may apply for a utility patent for "any new and useful process, article of manufacture or composition of matter." In order to patent a drink, it must be novel, "non-obvious," and adequately and clearly described in the patent application. A bartender can search the U.S. Patent and Trademark Office's database to check if their desired drink name or recipe is available, but they must understand that the contents of patents can be freely viewed by the public, so their drink recipe would hardly be a secret.

While it is typically difficult to copyright or patent a beverage recipe or trademark a beverage name, the addition of NFTs to the mix might be a digital game changer for cocktail and even beer recipes. With drink specialists "minting" their recipes in an NFT, the ownership and provenance of their creations will be instantly verifiable on the blockchain, and they will be able to sell the NFTs to generate income both on the first sale and in secondary transactions in perpetuity.

Funding for new ventures, campaigns, and projects has become a popular means for bringing tangible value to NFTs. Basing business investment and ventures in NFTs promises to democratize commercial opportunities. Several NFT-funding initiatives aim to accomplish three primary goals:

1. *Reducing the amount of capital required to partake in an investment*
2. *Expediting and streamlining the investment workflow so small investors can capitalize*
3. *Improving communication to educate potential investors regarding transaction costs and other conditions*

Non-fungible Funding:
Using NFTs for Crowdfunding

Recently, more and more companies are looking to leverage non-fungible tokens (NFTs) to generate funding. NFTs' adaptability, flexibility, and structure allow for the authenticated transfer of ownership of unique goods on the blockchain and

make them a viable alternative to traditional and corporate venture capital, debt financing, and equity sales as a means for raising capital. NFTs can be made or minted from almost anything—a digital image of a sneaker, an athlete, or even a tweet. However, these and other characteristics inherent in NFTs can create complications. This article examines the legal considerations that businesses should keep in mind before using NFTs for crowdfunding or raising capital.

Background

Crowdfunding campaigns, whether equity- or non-equity-based, invite people to participate by contributing money to help an enterprise reach specific campaign goals such as building a prototype, launching a product, or creating a marketing campaign. These acts of participation can be encoded as NFTs that document the contributions and are owned by everyone who invests in the fundraising campaign. Recently, not-for-profits such as UNICEF and the World Wildlife Fund have used NFTs for fundraising. UNICEF has launched 1,000 NFTs to celebrate the United Nations' 75th anniversary and to raise money and awareness for education and children's charities. For-profit businesses can adopt similar tactics to secure capital from NFTs. However, they should keep in mind several key legal considerations.

NFTs as Securities

The Securities and Exchange Commission (SEC) is investigating whether the use of NFTs to raise money can closely resemble—and therefore should be regulated as—traditional securities. To determine whether an NFT falls under the definition of "security," regulators apply the seminal guidelines established in *SEC v. Howey*. In this decision, the US Supreme Court laid out a four-prong test (subsequently known as the 'Howey Test') for determining whether a transaction qualifies as an "investment contract" and is thus subject to disclosure and registration requirements under the Securities Act of 1933 and the Securities Exchange Act of 1934:

1. Is there an investment of money?
2. Does the NFT represent a common enterprise?
3. Do contributors invest with the expectation of earning profits?
4. Would those profits accrue solely from the efforts of others?

Answering "yes" to all four questions would categorize an NFT as an investment contract subject to SEC laws. It is easy to see how NFTs used for crowdfunding purposes could fall under this definition. It is recommended to consult a securities lawyer experienced in the NFT space to determine whether compliance with securities law is necessary to raise money via NFTs.

NFTs as Collateral

One of the biggest advantages of using NFTs for crowdfunding or other fundraising activities is their status as collateral for securing loans. Like other secured loans, if the borrower fails to pay back the loan, the lender can seize the collateral. With NFT loans, however, the NFT owner offers his or her token as collateral to borrow money in the form of ERC20 tokens, stablecoins, other cryptocurrencies, or fiat currency. If the borrower fails to pay back the loan, the borrower risks forfeiting ownership of the NFT. In the event the borrower defaults, the NFT will be transferred to the lender, who becomes the new owner. In general, any default should be advantageous for the lender as the amount lent should always be less than the value of the NFT.

Currently, few platforms facilitate startups' efforts to raise capital via NFTs. As the trend toward NFT loans grows, however, several established platforms are becoming involved. One such platform is Arcade which provides private individuals and startup companies a means to raise capital from independent lenders and angel investors by using NFTs as collateral. The idea is to give people holding significant NFT collections a way to leverage them for investment without forcing them to sell their digital assets outright. The borrowing terms and conditions vary from platform to platform.

NFTs to Attract Investors and Maximize Investor Value

On a very broad level, startup founders hope to achieve three major goals: attracting investors, increasing market share, and maximizing exit value. NFTs can assist entrepreneurs in furthering one or more of those goals. A video game startup, for instance, could use NFTs to limit and track the distribution of its software. By authenticating ownership of the intellectual property tied to the NFT, the company can distinguish pirated software from legitimate, licensed versions. This can be used to protect and increase revenue to the benefit of both the company and its shareholders. Startups, particularly those selling software, may wish to leverage NFTs as temporary substitutes for formal intellectual property protection. At the same time, it is important to understand that NFTs cannot replace traditional copyright and trademark protections and do not grant ownership over the underlying content unless explicitly stated in their terms of sale or licensing.

Any business or startup can use NFTs to raise money. The notification issued by the SEC on NFTs as securities suggests that the definition of a security under US law can be quite broad. However, commentators have suggested that the basic logic behind the Howey Test should not apply to digital assets such as NFTs. In light of unsettled business and legal questions, emerging technologies companies intending to use NFTs to raise money for their business should consult a lawyer to ensure that their use of NFTs does not run afoul of US securities laws and regulations. SEC Commissioner Hester Peirce has cautioned that certain digital assets can be considered investment products and thus subject to US securities law. This is a legal gray area and companies should proceed carefully.

The importance of positioning brand- and product-linked NFTs as a container of intrinsic value was driven home just days after this article was written in July 2022. That's when it was revealed that Bored Ape Yacht Club was facing a class-action lawsuit alleging it used celebrity endorsements to inflate the NFTs' prices by touting their growth prospects and the potential for extraordinary returns on investment. If a court decides Yuga's NFTs are securities, the company would be in violation of laws requiring disclosures and registration. The same week the planned lawsuit surfaced, the SEC announced an investigation into Coinbase for allegedly listing crypto tokens that could be considered securities. None of those questionable listings are NFTs, however.

As Good as Advertised? NFTs in Marketing

Non-fungible tokens (NFTs) are quickly establishing themselves as one of the fastest growing and most innovative advertising media. "NFT" is now a key marketing buzzword,

with Collins Dictionary naming it the 2021 Word of the Year.

From just $95 million in 2020, the NFT market exploded in 2021, reaching a total sales volume of $25 billion. This article will discuss how emerging technology companies and even mainstream consumer brands can engage their consumers through NFT marketing.

NFT marketing, too, has come to the fore as regulators struggle to find ways to protect consumers and bring a semblance of order to the NFT space. Businesses exploring ways to use NFTs in their marketing programs should take care that their tokens are not issued to create an expectation of profit to the buyer based on the efforts of others. Beyond that caveat, an attorney experienced with digital assets and technology regulation can assist businesses in their efforts to leverage the power of NFT marketing.

NFTs, like other digital assets, include metadata and security codes embedded in cryptographic authentication and blockchain technology. These digital works of art, collectibles, video and audio clips, virtual real estate, gaming resources, and other "property" may or may not include the right to leverage the intellectual property or "real-world" entity they represent. Those that do carry tangible benefits that extend well beyond any speculative value that may or may not be realized due to market sentiment. These NFTs also are more likely to remain on the unregulated side of the playing field if the Securities and Exchange Commission or another nation's regulators decide that some NFTs behave as securities and therefore should be monitored and taxed as such.

Create a Story by Connecting NFT to your Brand
There is always a story behind everything brands attempt to accomplish. Many brands try to engage users through Discord or other onboarding platforms. However, they may quickly realize that it is better to understand their audience and its identity. Originality is key. Engage your audience by telling a story it can relate to. Cryptocurrency/ NFTs are not only for hardcore users. When you speak their language, people will love it too. They enable companies to tell their story using controlled, managed messaging that delivers several benefits:

- Establishing intimate, emotional, and personal connections with the community
- Empowering customers by giving them a say in the brand's mission and direction
- Ending to the "fake it 'til you make it" mentality by demonstrating authenticity and exclusivity
- Rewarding loyal customers for their time and effort
- Engaging followers with the company's vision, leadership, and raison d'etre

In today's digital age, NFTs go beyond collectibles and art. For example, OG Esports dropped its third NFT at Binance. In place of trading cards, the organization used NFTs to tell the story of an OG astronaut's landing on Binance. A pioneer of Esports organizations, OG Esports understands how NFTs can benefit their followers. The release of fan tokens and other NFT-related projects allows OG Esports to interact with its community more effectively and generate more revenue.

Use NFTs to Leverage Their Marketing Utility

Brands reach a wider audience by joining NFT marketplaces. These diverse communities composed of digital creators, art collectors, young and experienced entrepreneurs, and a wide range of other participants are eager to engage, thanks to NFTs' novelty and real-world profit potential As brands create more NFTs, they raise their profiles in the community and quickly become part of the conversation. The customer base will expand, presenting a larger pool of potential buyers that increases the likelihood of closing a sale. Brands can connect with their audience through NFTs in a way that no other marketing medium can provide.

A successful brand's marketing contributes to its legacy, distinguishing temporary fads from long-term successes. Look at NFTs as a medium (with lots of utilities) for the marketing message and delivery mechanism, rather than being the message itself.

Video game producers, extended reality content generators, musicians, artists, and digital transformers can use NFTs as part of their marketing efforts, advertisements, analytical tools, billboards, and other marketing media. This is one of the best ways to leverage NFTs to create long-term business value.

Mobilizing NFTs in Marketing

NFTs are far more than jpeg images linked to blockchains—they provide utility to your audience and brand strategy. Savvy brands follow marketing best practices to squeeze the most value from their NFT campaigns:

- Identifying the audience's inner thoughts and feelings, not just its demographics

- Performing due diligence to protect their own and avoid infringing on others' intellectual property rights

- Using a story to connect the brand to the audience

- Making the story and the brand accessible across channels

As an example of doing things right, Warner Bros. used the Nifty social NFT platform to announce the availability of avatars via blockchain to promote the fourth installment in its successful Matrix franchise, *The Matrix: Resurrections*. With the NFT collection, fans could choose to keep their avatar in the matrix by swallowing the "Blue Pill" or becoming a resistance fighter by choosing the "Red Pill." It proved a great way to generate hype and engage fans and customers around the film's premiere.

Like buying physical action figures or baseball cards, the process allows the original consumers to sell or trade their avatars, creating scarcity and value.

Monitor the Market and Maintain Authenticity

For marketers contemplating their first foray into NFTs and Web3, this new space may seem daunting. Observing what works and pitfalls trip up early adopters can help brands figure out how to proceed. This new paradigm favors the bold, offering immeasurable rewards for earnest adoption and experimentation than did earlier iterations of web technology. But consumers can spot a fraud a mile away. Trying to appear part of a community by co-opting NFT protocols in social media posts may backfire, making brands seem out of touch and token NFT art collection efforts will probably not resonate any more than dot-com era vanity websites.

Fortunately, the NFT universe will coalesce over the next few years, so there's plenty of time for emerging media and technology firms to figure out how to incorporate them into their marketing tactics. A business's prospective NFT customers should include not just the crypto community, but anyone who could benefit from the products and services offered. The prices a commercial concern's NFTs fetch on OpenSea shouldn't be the measure of the company's success. Instead, they should focus on metrics that can better illustrate a future in which NFTs anchor all real-world products and experiences with digital extensions.

What Is the Value of NFTs in Marketing?

Brands may have difficulty selling NFTs because they are risky. The future is unclear, and it is too early to estimate their impact. But many of those who have used it have seen great success.

Based on HubSpot Blog Research, 39 percent of NFT users say their NFTs have the highest ROI among their advertising investments. More than one in seven say they plan to use NFTs for the first time in 2022. Brands benefit from more trackable incentives through Web3 and NFTs. The brand and goals will determine whether this is valuable. One thing is sure, though: It's definitely worth watching.

Similar to DeFi lending, NFT owners can earn passive income by staking their tokens on a blockchain platform. Staking earns owners compensation for allowing their NFTs to be used by cryptocurrency mining platforms to use them as proof of stake to support its operations. Like a certificate of deposit at a bank, the amount of reward depends on the platform's rates, the length of time owners are willing to lock up their NFT, and the unit or quantity of NFT being staked. Many NFT owners take this approach to earn passive income instead of selling their NFTs, which disposes of their assets and often takes time to complete (the "illiquidity" problem).

Sell the Sizzle, Not the Stake: Marketing NFTs

Numerous celebrities, musicians, athletes, and other influencers have invested in NFT artwork and technology, whether for their personal use or for building the next stage of their brand and empire. Concurrently, NFTs have evolved from the exclusive domain of digital artists to become major marketing tools for companies like Twitter and Warner Bros.

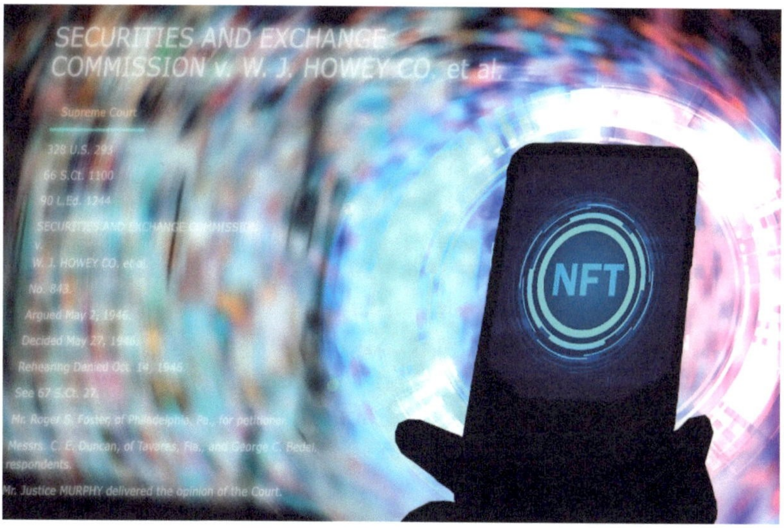

Investors and consumers alike have been captured by the non-fungible token craze, which skyrocketed in 2021 with about $44 billion worth of crypto sent to NFT smart contracts on the Ethereum blockchain—an exponential increase from 2020's $106 million. Sales reached a record high of $6.13 billion in January 2022 before coming back to Earth in the following months.

Still in its nascent stages, the NFT market presents some real legal and regulatory issues that are complicated by confusing jurisdictions and the application of laws designed for more traditional investments and technologies. Some investors and attorneys deem NFTs to be shielded from securities and investment laws, but other fintech lawyers and Securities and Exchange (SEC) experts warn that NFTs are increasingly blurring the lines.

NFTs Are Not Considered Securities…Yet

NFTs are typically thought of as collectibles, like pieces of art or baseball cards, and they are non-fungible, meaning that each NFT is a one-of-a-kind asset. NFT creators can set the sales price and the maximum number of items that can be produced, as well as explicitly state which, if any, licenses NFT ownership conveys, and how royalties are to be paid in their smart contracts.

Transactions involving NFTs don't need intermediaries for sales because they can be sold peer-to-peer or in an NFT marketplace. However, NFTs can be linked to a variety of aesthetic and intangible assets, including digital art, video clips, and game items. They are registered on the blockchain and possess their own unique, digital "fingerprint." NFTs can also be tied to other assets that can be digital or physical as determined in the smart contract. Use cases to date have included physical art pieces, rare wines, concert performances, real estate, and more.

Initially, NFTs were marketed and sold as single lots but now more are being fractionalized to allow for shared ownership. What might have begun as a single collectible now may start to look like a security or share of stock in an investment, especially when the NFTs lean towards more brand-based collections. While NFTs are non-fungible, the smart contracts tied to them and the terms contained therein may make them less fungible by adding fractional ownership provisions where one "share" of an NFT accrues the same royalties, profit sharing, and profit upon resale as any other share. If an NFT transaction triggers cryptocurrency or security regulation, creators and owners may need to demonstrate that the assets involved are non-fungible in order to avoid legal hot water and unfavorable tax treatment.

Non-fungibility and the ability to pass the three-pronged Howey test are not always mutually exclusive. The process is case-specific and the devil is in the details when it comes to determining whether an asset is an investment contract. Howey indicates that something is a security when the purchaser invests money in a common enterprise with the expectation of making profits through the efforts of someone else. The Howey test applies to any contract, scheme, or transaction regardless of whether it appears to be a traditional security.

NFT Staking

Staking NFTs has become more popular in recent years. Staking is a way to put a unique NFT on the blockchain and into the marketplace. When an NFT is staked, it's attached to a platform or protocol. In exchange for allowing his or her NFT to be used as "proof of stake" (POS) in crypto mining operations, the NFT creator earns rewards as well as other unique benefits.

NFTs can also be staked in similar fashion as cryptocurrency. Using a smart contract or appropriate blockchain protocol and a suitable crypto wallet, NFT stakers lend their assets and in return receive a percentage of their worth (similar to bond investing) and other benefits as determined in the relevant smart contract. The owners retain ownership of the NFT and reclaim possession at the end of the contracted staking period.

While NFT staking is still in its infancy stage, it functions as a key bridge between NFTs and the DeFi economy. With the growing popularity of NFT staking, owners need to be aware of potential securities issues. Staking could be considered a securities scheme (failing the Howey test) unless the NFTs involved demonstrate utility and the marketing is aimed at that utility rather than the possibility of financial gain. The SEC has begun to investigate certain crypto exchanges for violating its rules. BlockFi received a $100 million fine for failing to register products it uses to pay customers for putting their digital tokens up for lease. In particular, the SEC is gathering information regarding fractional NFTs to determine where exactly they fall on the regulatory spectrum.

Keeping NFTs in the Non-Security Realm

Investors and minters interested in NFTs should be aware of growing government scrutiny of NFTs, including the staking and fractionalization of NFTs. Most whole, unique NFTs assets are unlikely to be considered securities. However, fractional NFTs will likely receive closer scrutiny by the SEC for appearing and acting more like securities than traditional NFTs, especially if the owners are expected to receive profits, the money is used to build a platform, or if the NFT acts a license to another digital asset and will receive a share of attributed revenues. Marketing fractional NFTs as assets that will generate profits places emphasis on the potential for investment returns based on the NFT promoter's ongoing efforts as compared to the consumptive value of the NFT as a digital asset.

Owners and creators of NFTs will want to avoid financial penalties and reputational damage from violating SEC rules. Working with an attorney who understands the current and upcoming regulatory conditions can help NFT creators and owners avoid potentially violating SEC rules and enjoy their unique digital assets.

The prospect of big revenue accruing to NFT development deals can lead some to put the cart before the horse. Any organization contemplating an NFT deal should thoroughly vet the companies, developers, marketers, sales agents, and other partners involved. Failure to perform this due diligence can create a situation in which a signatory takes on more responsibility than it has the resources to accomplish. In other cases, contradictory or incomplete contract terms can allow critical tasks to go unfulfilled. In this case, Bondly was under the impression that G2 Esports was responsible for conceptualizing, scaling, and implementing its NFT strategy. G2, on the other hand, contends that performing these tasks was one of the primary reasons it engaged Bondly.

When NFT Deals Go Bad: Lessons from G2 v. Bondly

With Non-fungible tokens (NFTs) comprising a multi-million-dollar market, there is seemingly no limit to their potential—the summer 2022 slump notwithstanding. Though some NFTs sell for millions of dollars and make their creators

rich overnight, most NFTs sell for much more modest prices. Bloomberg estimates the average NFT can be had for just under $2,000. While NFTs don't necessarily offer a "get rich quick" scheme anymore, they can provide significant revenues for brand owners, artists, and minters. Companies can use NFTs to promote their products, events, or brands. NFTs no longer are the exclusive domain of digital art collectors and video gamers; they have since branched out into other collectible spaces, notably for entertainment, music, and esports. This rapid expansion has created growing pains for some participants. As G2 Esports recently discovered, forging partnerships with the wrong collaborators or if they fail to address each party's rights and responsibilities, problems are bound to arise.

When Deals Go Sideways: G2 Esports v. Bondly

In March 2022, G2 Esports filed a lawsuit against Bondly in Los Angeles Superior Court claiming intellectual property rights violations and seeking damages. G2 alleges that Bondly breached its contract to develop and promote a series of NFTs based on G2 Esports' intellectual property relating to the company and esports teams it sponsors.

The plaintiff is a European e-sports entertainment company that brings together industry-leading brands and players to compete in League of Legends, Valorant, Counter-Strike: Global Offensive, Hearthstone, Rocket League, Rainbow Six Siege, and iRacing esports leagues. The defendant, Bondly (since rebranded as Forj), is a blockchain technology company that creates NFTs based on music, entertainment, gaming, and collectibles and administers a suite of products and services that support the blockchain ecosystem.

In the lawsuit, G2 asserts that Bondly misled the company leadership about its NFT-creating abilities and missed key deadlines for deliverables and payments. The parties entered into an exclusive two-year contract in June 2021 under which Bondly agreed to develop NFTs for G2 Esports and to function as its agent and promoter. In exchange, Bondly would pay G2 a series of fees for its intellectual property rights, which it planned to recoup through sales of the NFTs.

The agreement granted Bondly access to G2 Esport's intellectual property, including images, video, and audio files. Shortly after G2 sent the first rights-fee invoice to Bondly, it says it discovered that Bondly would not be able to deliver the NFTs as promised. The parties could not agree on who was responsible for certain deliverables and tasks as outlined in the contract. Bondly later attempted to end the contract, citing G2's unwillingness to compromise. Claiming breach of contract because of the non-payment and non-delivery of the NFTs, G2 filed suit seeking $5.25 million—two years' worth of $2 million in annual rights fees and the agreed-upon advance guarantee of $1.25 million. The case highlights potential problems surrounding NFT partnerships when licensing, distribution, and other rights and responsibilities are not clearly delineated in the contract.

Web 3.0 partnerships

The G2 Esports/Bondly case highlights the key considerations in Web 3.0 world partnerships. Web 3.0 would not be possible without collaboration between diverse players bringing complementary skills and resources to the ecosystem. Any partnership agreement to create NFTs will clearly need to spell out rights, responsibilities, and any other pertinent factors in order to make these partnerships run smoothly. When entering a contract for an NFT, it is recommended to cover several considerations:

- ***Intellectual property rights***—NFTs should be considered intellectual property, subject to copyright protection and design patent rights. NFT creators often stipulate in their sales contract that they retain the copyright to their underlying assets. Copyrights on NFTs exist as soon as they are created, and copyright ownership does not necessarily transfer when the NFT is sold.

- ***Trademark extension***—Brand owners should extend their trademark rights to cover additional uses, including technologies and media not yet in existence. These provisions will reserve owners' rights to exploit NFT and other digital uses of their products' images. Several well-known brands, including Nike and Hermes have learned this lesson the hard way and were forced to assert their brand autonomy in court.

- ***Royalty rates***—Because copyrights attach to NFTs, creators can specify royalty payments in the smart contracts governing their use. For each sale, the creator can receive a portion of that sale going forward. NFT owners will receive their share of the sale price.

- ***Licenses***—NFT purchasers should engage an attorney experienced in licensing, IP, and digital technology to review licenses that call for the reproduction of copyrighted content. Most NFT licenses only grant the buyer limited capacity to use, copy, and display the NFT. They usually cannot commercialize the NFT by creating derivative content or using the NFT to market a product or company. If that is the intent, buyers should negotiate those rights and be prepared to pay extra for the privilege. These expanded rights are becoming more common with the success enjoyed by Bored Ape Yacht Club and Cryptokitties.

- ***Design patents***—Brand owners should become conversant with how current and future design patents can protect their interests against counterfeits or infringement, so they will know how to protect their assets, enforce their rights, and recover damages. While NFTs cannot be duplicated due to their unique "fingerprint" on the blockchain that verifies their authenticity, they can be replicated.

- ***Securities designation***—The Securities and Exchange Commission does not currently consider NFTs securities, but there is a growing movement within regulatory communities to revisit this policy. Owners should be aware if the SEC decides an NFT is marketed based on potential profits accruing to buyers based on the efforts of others they could satisfy the "Howey test" and be categorized as investment contracts. Additionally, the fractionalization of NFTs has raised eyebrows and could lead them to be regarded as unregistered securities and sanctioned and taxed accordingly.

- ***Private personal data***—Several high-profile breaches have brought data security into the public eye, and governments in the US, Europe, and Asia have taken steps to mandate higher-level protection. These laws could potentially cover NFTs. Any NFT agreement should include a personal private data policy to ensure that no NFT contains sensitive data or, if it does, how its security will be maintained.

The legal rules and regulations surrounding NFTs and the blockchain are still evolving, so partnerships in Web 3.0 will have to adapt as the law eventually catches up to the new technology. To avoid litigation, any NFT agreement should consider the rights of each party in the partnership, who's in charge of marketing, which platform to sell the NFTs, and the blockchain to use as well as intellectual property and passive income streams. Companies that want to avoid poor collaboration choices as befell G2 Esports should understand the potential pitfalls and plan accordingly. A consultation with an attorney specializing in the blockchain/NFT space and well-versed in contract law could prove valuable.

Around the time this article was published, Tennessee became the second state to include DAOs among the business structures it would recognize. The Tennessee legal code now allows the state's limited liability companies to register as "decentralized organizations" simply by including "the company is a decentralized organization" or similar language in their articles of organization, thus providing their members the same protections against seizure of personal assets as those enjoyed by participants in traditional LLCs. The amended law requires smart contract-managed DAOs to include amendable contracts and publicly available identifiers.

Do's and DAOn'ts: Setting Up a DAO For Your NFT Project

Decentralized autonomous organizations (DAOs) are increasingly popular as the organizational structure of choice for many individuals, groups, and companies pursuing NFT-based projects and businesses. In this article, we delve into the legal considerations that NFT ventures should keep in mind while setting up their own DAOs.

What Are DAOs? Why Are They Important for NFTs?

DAOs are organizations governed by rules encoded as computer algorithms to ensure transparent operations and transactions controlled by the organization's members rather than an elevated group such as a board of directors or C-level executives. These community coalitions use tokens to represent voting power, as decided by the size of each member's investment or work performed to further its development or objectives. DAOs use smart contracts to automatically execute commands whenever a set of conditions are met. For instance, these contracts may trigger payments, authorize transactions, or initiate a course of action when a majority of the voting stock is cast in favor of a particular action.

The rules of a DAO are stored on an open source blockchain, so anyone can look into the code and view the transaction records, but they cannot alter the code unless conditions are met that instruct the smart contract to do so. Since there is no central authority that can direct decisions in a DAO, members can share proposals and potential projects within the community where they may be adopted according to the vote. DAOs function similarly to corporations, but without the hierarchical structure. Their primary advantage is in promoting a flat, democratic process through decentralized governance. Unlike a traditional corporation or similar organization, members of a DAO are not bound by any formal contract. Instead, they share a goal or a joint purpose written into rules. There are many different types of DAOs.

Legal Considerations for DAOs

Any project or business utilizing a DAO should perform due diligence and seek the advice of an attorney experienced in the digital space to ensure compliance and protections afforded by law. There are several variables to consider.

- ***Legal Status***—DAOs are not recognized as legal entities in the vast majority of US states and are not expected to comply with registration provisions in these states. Only Wyoming and Vermont extend DAOs corporate privileges such as limited liability that are usually available to traditionally incorporated entities. The other 48 states and the District of Columbia may even exclude DAOs from entering certain commercial contracts with other entities or the government, due to their lack of legal status.

- ***Asset Protection***—Unlike corporate shareholders, DAO members do not generally enjoy financial protections if their organization is sued. This is because DAOs are unincorporated entities and are not subject to the legal formalities of incorporation such as registration, bylaws, and contracts. Instead, they are treated as partnerships in which each member assumes joint and several liability. Therefore, if the DAO is hacked, declares bankruptcy, or owes money it cannot repay, each member is responsible for making creditors whole, exposing their personal assets. To address this weakness, a DAO would have to register and be recognized as an LLC or LLP.

- ***Regulatory Framework***—Because many states treat DAOs as partnerships, not only are their members exposed to personal liability, but other legal risks are created as well. For example, regulatory inconsistencies may lead to investigations into financial and asset trading violations. A report issued by the Securities Exchange Commission (SEC) in 2017 concluded that a DAO that sells tokens without properly registering them may violate multiple federal laws.

- ***AML/KYC policies***—Many traditional corporate entities are subject to anti-money laundering and know-your-customer (AML/KYC) policies that prescribe safeguards organizations must implement to ensure they deal only with legitimate partners, customers, and token holders. The rules also require verification of members' identities and reporting of certain financial transactions. DAOs often are formed precisely to allow their members to remain anonymous; reconciling this advantage with AML/KYC policies becomes complicated, considering DAO memberships can include individuals from around the world. Deciding which country's laws apply can be difficult and is likely to result in protracted legal battles if a dispute arises.

- **Decision-Making and Dispute Resolution**—Decision-making in a DAO is conducted by voting by its members. This means that each member of the DAO can influence its actions or future by initiating a new governance or management proposal themselves. This is in sharp contrast to traditional corporations where decision-making is centralized and the final authority to make decisions rests solely with the senior management, shareholders, or a board. The aforementioned jurisdictional issues can make resolving disputes a tricky proposition.

From the above, it is clear that there are a number of legal risks and considerations involved in creating a DAO in the US. There are jurisdictions friendlier than the US for DAOs such as the Cayman Islands, British Virgin Islands, El Salvador, Singapore, and Gibraltar. It is best to consult a corporate attorney with a current understanding of DAOs and related developments to check whether a DAO is the correct legal structure for your organization.

Conclusion

DAOs are taking the NFT world by storm as the next generation of financial and business innovation. They offer many advantages over traditional corporations including decen-tralization, member-driven voting and decision-making, and pooling of funds. Nonetheless, they pose many legal risks as they are not generally recognized as legal entities in the US. Further, DAOs that involve multiple jurisdictions may complicate compliance for parties using NFTs. It is best to consult a law firm specializing in legal structures for emerging technologies organizations to reap the benefits of a DAO without falling foul of potential legal risks and pitfalls.

COURT CASES AND REGULATORY ACTIONS

The "original" NFT license developed by Dapper Labs was a significant step toward standardizing and delineating the rights that come with purchasing NFTs. However, the personal use and limited commercial rights outlined in it do not provide a one-size-fits-all solution. Often, intellectual property holders do not want to convey no creative rights to the purchaser. On the other hand, NFT miners may generate higher sales prices by permitting purchasers to profit from derivative creations based on the original artwork. When some but not all commercial rights come with the NFT, organizations should employ comprehensive licensing agreements that not only specify what the buyer can do with the NFT but also what uses are expressly forbidden.

Essential Considerations in NFT Licensing Agreements

Technology has changed the way the world generates, grows, stores, and maintains value. The concept of "asset" has evolved from strictly tangible exchange media to digital property such as cryptocurrency and non-fungible tokens

(NFTs). Digital assets are the latest trend, occupying the thoughts – and wallets – of a growing number of buyers, investors, and speculators. While many remain convinced that crypto represents the future of legal tender, experts are less sanguine about the prospects for NFTs. To be sure, there is a lot of money to be made in the NFT market, but how to approach these opportunities and how to manage risk are critical considerations in any NFT business dealing.

Issues Surrounding NFT Offerings

NFTs have opened the door for people all around the world to convert their artwork, collectibles, and other original creations into revenue-generating digital property. Because NFTs have become a global phenomenon, numerous jurisdictions have promulgated diverse rules governing their use, sale, and distribution. The monetization of NFTs often must conform to financial, legal, and contractual guidelines, that vary depending on where the deals are struck. In most cases, jurisdictions base their NFT copyright guidelines on European Research Council rule no. 721 (ERC-721) blockchain smart contract standard. Under this standard, creators and owners of unique crypto assets (UCAs) can verify the digital scarcity of their possession by recording it on the Ethereum public distributed ledger, where UCAs can be stored and transferred. The technology provides UCA holders in copyright-intensive disciplines such as gaming collectibles with certain intellectual property rights protection and authority over their NFT-backed creations.

However, some questions linger over the relationship between artists, collectors, investors, and licensors. Since these artworks have subjective value and cannot be sold off in pieces (the essence of "non-fungibility,") the question of how NFT transactions should be regulated, taxed, and policed remains unanswered. Other questions surround the relationship between an NFT backing an asset and the asset itself. Unlike cryptocurrencies, which are governed by financial regulations, the assets associated with NFTs contain aesthetic value as well as monetary value, muddying the regulatory waters and subjecting them to consumer protection, truth-in-advertising, and other aspects of the law in addition to IP and investment law:

- Can, and if so, how, an NFT's investment value be distinguished from its intrinsic value?
- How should the transfer – sale, gift, inheritance – of NFTs be regulated and treated for tax purposes?
- What rights do NFT owners have, vis-à-vis the original creation on which the NFT is based?

These are all questions an experienced intellectual property and blockchain attorney should be engaged to answer. A lawyer specializing in crypto transactions and IP law can be a critical resource to navigate the jurisdictional and contractual issues to advise NFT owners, licensees, and buyers on their rights and responsibilities.

NFT Licensing

By most reckonings, a person owns an NFT if he or she has rightfully purchased it from or been assigned by a legitimate source, as documented and recorded on the relevant blockchain.

In cases where the original creator or owner of the tangible artwork or collectible maintains ownership even after someone else purchases the associated NFT, licensing agreements must specify exactly which rights each holds, and what the NFT owners can and cannot do with a digital certificate. Most NFT licensing agreements contain several standard clauses:

1. Whether the buyer or licensee may transfer the permissions to a third party, and if so, whether and how the original creator will be compensated.

2. How the NFT may be used, such as in advertisements, marketing campaigns, promotions, or merchandising.

3. If the NFT can be copied and sold (similar to numbered prints of an original painting). If so, how will the revenue be split between the licensee and the creator?

4. Whether the NFT owner can create derivative or modified versions, and how he or she can use them.

Creator Protections

NFT license agreements were developed to protect creators' intellectual property rights and enable them to profit from their talent and assets. Cryptokitties, one of the pioneers in the NFT trade, developed the first licensing agreement and set the standard for future deals. The Cryptokitties licensing contract accomplished its stated goal of establishing "a framework for blockchain developers to establish sustainable businesses and offer them a secure path to monetization, much like the App Store did for early third-party developers...The NFT License is a first step in determining what it will mean to own digital assets."

NFT license agreements are executed and stored in blockchain-enabled smart contracts. This allows the autonomous code to also execute resales and manage monetary transfers. Some smart contracts call for the originator to receive a portion of the proceeds from every resale. These transactions can be tricky, and creators and buyers should take care that the license contains precise, legally binding language and that all parties understand the revenue-sharing or royalty model being used. An attorney experienced in blockchain and digital media can ensure everyone's interests are addressed.

Know the Risks

As with virtually any investment, purchasing NFT licenses carries several types of risks; some involve the market while others center on the transaction and the platform:

- Platform unreliability and inaccuracies
- Tax liabilities stemming from NFT ownership
- Potential for detrimental changes in blockchain, crypto, and NFT regulation
- Token availability, storage issues
- Market volatility

Your attorney can advise you of the risks involved and help structure NFT license agreements to mitigate the risk, protect your interests, and create licenses that clearly outline the rights and responsibilities of NFT minters and purchasers.

While no jurisdiction has adopted any comprehensive regulations or classifications for NFTs since the publication of this article in mid-2021, the United States and the European Union have taken steps to distinguish between ancillary NFTs and other digital assets and those that constitute e-money or value-referenced tokens. According to the US's Responsible Financial Innovation Act and EU's Markets in Crypto-Assets regulation both recognize the difference between NFTs that convey "non-securitization" rights as defined by the Howey Test (according to RFIA) and those that are intended merely to prove ownership or give holders digital access to goods or services provided by the NFT issuer (according to MiCA).

Legal and Regulatory Challenges For Non-fungible Assets

One of the hottest trends of 2021, non-fungible tokens (NFTs) have empowered a new generation of digital artists and turned many speculators and creators into millionaires and overnight celebrities. NFTs are also gaining traction in the video games industry thanks to their ability to solve problems

such as the creation, management, and sale of rare commodities. NFTs are frequently used to grant players - rather than the game developer - ownership of their in-game assets. Assets created, found, mined, grown, bought, traded, and even plundered in-game can be transported across platforms and sold in real-life. Beyond the art and gaming world, NFTs are also used for verifying identity, ticketing, tokenizing physical property, and other practical functions. NFTs are unique, scarce, durable, and extendable. While there is no shortage of information about the advantages that NFTs bring to digital transactions and activities, there are several legal, regulatory, environmental, and operational challenges that must be overcome for businesses and organizations to take full advantage of this potentially game-changing technology.

Intellectual Property

As NFT applications expand beyond cryptocurrencies and into new industries, not everyone involved in the buying and selling of assets attached to them fully understands what they are dealing with. Possession of an NFT does not automatically grant ownership of the underlying artwork or another asset. An NFT merely grants the buyer the right to use the creative output or object it represents for their personal use. For example, if someone buys an NFT tied to a painting, he or she merely has gained the right to display the digital art in their token wallet. They will not have the right to reproduce, create derivative works, or sell prints or copies of the painting. From a copyright perspective, an NFT is simply a digital receipt indicating ownership of a particular *version* of the artwork.

Given the immature market and spotty regulation of NFTs, criminals have already found ways to use them to steal intellectual property. Several prominent digital artists have seen their work sold as NFTs without their permission and have voiced concern that once their digital art has been hijacked and inscribed in a blockchain-enabled token, they will lose ownership over their work. While the tokens can be sold, art can only be tokenized legally with the artist's permission. Artists' concerns over losing copyright to creative output is unfounded, but the inherent difficulty in proving the place of origin of a piece of digital art places NFTs in a legal gray area for non-experts.

Jurisdictional Issues

A principal idea behind blockchain technology that underpins NFTs is that the ledger is not centrally located or managed. While this makes it nearly impossible to reverse-engineer or fabricate transactions, it also poses a complex jurisdictional challenge, as the lack of a specific governing locale makes it subject to different and often conflicting legal frameworks. The problem posed by conflicting laws is especially important from the perspective of copyright and moral rights. For example, moral rights differ significantly among common law and civil law jurisdictions (especially those with Germanic and Napoleonic legal traditions). In France, moral rights are perpetual, inalienable, and imprescriptible while in the US, moral rights come with statutes of limitation. As a result, the rights of artists to their underlying artwork can differ from jurisdiction to jurisdiction, and in some cases, there may be no way to clearly determine applicable laws and select a legitimate forum to consider disputes involving NFTs.

Smart Contracts

One of the most striking features of blockchain technology and NFTs is the self-executing "smart contract." Smart contracts are sets of promises that are usually specified in a digital format that form the basis on which the parties perform their specific contractual duties. Due to their inherent uniqueness and complexity, it is difficult to say whether smart contracts fit into the legal framework governing traditional contract law. This is especially true in the United States, where no federal contract law exists. Further, at the time of this article (April 2021), there is no federal law or guidance explicitly defining the legality of smart contracts in the first place. The only exception to this is the Electronic Signatures in Global and National Commerce Act of 2000, which provides limited legal validity to smart contracts. The legal validity of smart contracts vis-à-vis NFTs, however, remains unclear, setting the stage for potentially lengthy litigation in the future.

Privacy Concerns

The security that NFTs provide in assuring anonymity between contractual parties is often hailed as one of the technology's greatest benefits. Nevertheless, this advantage is not guaranteed to continue. Some believe it is only a matter of time before the marked improvement in blockchain analytic tools will be able to reveal identities and terms. Analysis tools such as Chainalysis, Reactor, Elliptic, and others can already trace blockchain transactions. While most are used for purposes such as tracing fraud and money laundering over the blockchain, they have the potential to track confidential and sensitive information.

Consumer Protection

NFTs raise significant issues related to consumer rights. Issues such as assigning permission and responsibility for recording transactions, the legality of digital receipts, and anti-fraud and anti-money laundering procedures is critical, as many consumers have little concept of what they are buying and their rights and responsibilities in relation to NFTs. Since the legal status of NFTs as consumer goods is still evolving, many customers may be left in the lurch in the event that complications with transactions or ownership arise. This is especially pertinent since, unlike traditional bank and credit card transactions, there is no financial institution to intervene if the end-user incurs a loss due to hacks, fraud, or breach of security.

Financial and Business Challenges

Other logistical, legal, and financial challenges will need to be addressed before NFTs become universally accepted. First, most NFT transactions involve cryptocurrencies that are not legal tender in the US and are not backed by any central issuing authority or inherently valuable asset. Cryptocurrencies are regulated by individual states and presently there is no protection available to consumers in the event of fraud. Second, there are tax implications related to buying NFTs with cryptocurrencies. Many buyers and sellers are unaware that they may be obligated to pay steep taxes if they profit in cryptocurrency trades. Third, NFTs could run afoul of US sanctions law which prevents US residents or citizens from conducting business with individuals or entities operating in nations on which the US has placed economic or trade sanctions. Though there are some exceptions for the use of NFTs for artwork from sanctioned nations, buyers and sellers should consult a lawyer if they have any questions or doubts about the legality of an NFT transaction.

Operational Challenges

Despite the hype surrounding NFTs, operational problems also plague NFTs:

- They are based on decentralized networks which are not 100 percent user-friendly. This means verifying, promoting, purchasing, selling, and storing an NFT requires a basic understanding of blockchain technology. In fact, only sophisticated blockchain technology users can use NFTs effectively.

- For NFTs to be truly successful, they need to be as ubiquitous as smartphones.

- The speculative nature of NFTs may pose a challenge for the gaming industry because players may be inclined to buy and hold NFTs with an eye toward selling them in the future for a profit instead of using them within the gaming ecosystem.

As with cryptocurrencies, the legal challenges related to NFTs are likely to become more pronounced over the coming months as the media focuses more and more attention on the technology. It is important to consult an attorney before creating, launching, or buying an NFT as the regulatory framework is still evolving. An experienced attorney will be able to guide you on anti-money laundering regulations, tax implications, financial regulations, intellectual property issues, and the like. They can also prepare all the preliminary legal documents before you dive into the world of NFTs.

The move toward consistent global regulation of NFTs and other digital assets really picked up steam less than two weeks after this article originally appeared in late February 2022. Founded in the desire to counteract terrorism, money laundering, and fraud (and, let's be honest, to ensure they can collect taxes on NFT transactions) governments are cracking down on many of the features that make NFTs and the blockchain unique. Participant anonymity, opaque transactions, and under-the-radar deals have led regulators to target the industry. Investors have become justifiably skittish about what the future may bring. Anyone interested in minting, issuing, marketing, or investing in NFTs should educate themselves on the looming disclosure and tax requirements.

NFTs' 'Wild West' Days are Numbered: Global Regulation Looms

Driven by concerns over potential fraud, intellectual property theft, tax evasion, and money laundering, governments all around the world are looking at ways to regulate digital currencies and non-fungible tokens (NFTs). Nations have

taken vastly different approaches depending on who's in charge, how they characterize NFTs, and how bullish their outlook is on digital currencies. While some countries such as China have taken a more conservative approach, El Salvador, for example, made cryptocurrency legal tender last fall, in defiance of criticism from the International Monetary Fund (IMF). US President Joe Biden is now marshaling federal regulatory agencies in preparation for an executive order that will discuss crypto in terms of national security and law enforcement.

US Regulation of NFTs

In the US, NFTs have drawn significant regulatory scrutiny from multiple state and federal agencies since their popularity spiked in 2021. This is because the existing regulatory and legal environment is not designed to manage the creation, licensing, and trading of NFTs and other digital assets. While entrepreneurs have found novel ways to incorporate NFTs into esports, sports betting, film, and other industries, digital assets such as NFTs pose significant regulatory hurdles.

The White House's initial government-wide strategy to assess the risks and opportunities posed by cryptocurrencies and digital assets is seen as a sweeping first step toward defining regulatory approaches to NFTs. Research used to inform this strategy includes a Department of the Treasury report that details the impact of NFTs on money-laundering activities in the global art trade. According to the report, in certain circumstances, an NFT may be deemed a virtual asset service provider (VASP) under the Department of Treasury's Financial Crimes Enforcement Network's regulation (FinCEN). However, to date, FinCEN has not issued guidance specific to NFTs.

Given the complexities, gaps, and redundancies in the current regulations, it appears inevitable that Washington will issue additional guidance on how NFTs should be treated - as securities, currencies, collective investments, financial instruments, or something else. This is especially important since there is no single federal law that regulates digital assets. State regulation provides no consistent precedent.

Washington, D.C. and 49 states have at least one proposed or enacted regulation pertaining to digital assets and cryptocurrencies. At least 13 states have proposed or enacted legislation on licensing requirements, 25 have proposed or enacted a money transmitter law, and 23 have proposed or enacted bills to create a regulatory sandbox or committee to study the implementation and use of digital assets and cryptocurrencies. States typically focus on generating state revenue from NFTs and other digital assets, with 34 proposing or enacting tax regulations. These regulations vary widely from jurisdiction to jurisdiction and change frequently.

Scattershot enforcement of inconsistent law raises additional challenges:

- Litigation occurs one court at a time and leads to delayed and inconsistent decisions

- Enforcement matters that are settled do not carry any precedential effect

- Inconsistencies in the way in which enforcement matters are resolved can lead to conflicts between state and federal authorities

Europe

Regulators in Europe have taken an interest in digital assets though they have not yet expressly issued any regulations specific to NFTs. In 2020, the European Commission proposed a new regulation known as Markets-in-Crypto Assets (MiCA) to regulate virtual assets, streamline distributed ledger technology and provide legal certainty to digital assets such as cryptocurrencies, security tokens, and stablecoins. Certain provisions of the MiCA would apply to NFTs, due to the act's broad definition of the term "crypto-asset" which includes asset-referenced tokens, e-money tokens, and other digital assets. Under Title II of the MiCA Proposal, NFTs would likely fall into the "catch-all" category of "other crypto assets."

In addition to MiCA, some EU member states have issued regulations that specifically address NFTs. For example, Luxembourg recently grouped NFTs into three specific categories of collective investment instruments, electronic money, and financial instruments, each of which has its own respective qualities and regulations. Similarly, in 2019 France published the Law on Business Growth and Transformation (known as "PACTE") to comprehensively regulate crypto assets service providers ("CASPs").

Other Countries

There has been an increased drive by countries around the world to regulate digital assets. El Salvador recently doubled down on its commitment to Bitcoin, buying another $15 million worth during a recent plunge in the cryptocurrency's price. Still, the Central American nation has not yet promulgated guidelines to regulate digital assets, including NFTs. In February 2022, India announced a 30 percent tax on income derived from the transfer of any virtual assets. To capture details of applicable crypto transactions, India also will assess a 1 percent tax at the source on all such transactions. Similarly, Ukraine, Japan, Russia, Switzerland, and others have either devised rules to regulate digital assets or are in the process of regulating them. Conversely, China, for example, has taken a notoriously strict stance on cryptocurrencies, banning them outright. However, Chinese regulators are currently developing regulations governing and describing the legal minting, use, and trading of NFTs.

Conclusion

NFTs' arrival in the mainstream awareness and rapid proliferation has prodded nations around the world to increase their scrutiny to protect their citizens and collect their share of related revenue. With so much money at stake, we can expect even more regulation at the national and state levels. Government regulation is inevitable in most countries, as without a robust regulatory framework, there remains the growing risk of illegal activities such as tax evasion, money laundering, terrorist financing, fraud, and theft. NFTs have the potential to disrupt both existing and emerging technology sectors and drive commensurate opportunity and risk. Hence, businesses already using or considering taking advantage of this still-new technology must keep an eye on applicable regulatory developments.

Consultation with an experienced NFT attorney can help platforms, creators, and others in the NFT space comply with applicable law and navigate the complex and constantly evolving legal and regulatory landscape.

It was formerly the case that securities lawyers were generally comfortable advising clients that NFTs were likely not securities. NFTs are "non-fungible," after all, unlike stocks and bonds. And the SEC had not issued specific guidance that would suggest otherwise. However, not long after this article was written (August 2022), the SEC launched an investigation of Yuga Labs, apparently premised in part on the NFT apes being securities. At the time of this writing, there's been no specific guidance from the SEC on NFTs and when they could be considered securities.

Regulators Leaning toward Treating NFTs as Securities?

Recent legal developments in the US and elsewhere seem to point toward the eventual classification of NFTs as securities. Should the trend continue, these rulings and regulations are sure to have important consequences on the video game industry and on emerging technologies companies aiming to launch their own NFTs in the near future.

Background

Just how NFTs should be regarded by law enforcement, tax collectors, and financial regulators has been the subject of debate for almost as long as there have been NFTs. They can be owned, so are they private property? They have to be created, so are they art? They can be bought and sold freely on a number of markets, so are they commodities? And they can often accrue significantly higher value than their purchase price, so are they investments? Any digital asset, including NFTs, can be classified as "securities" by the US Securities and Exchange Commission or similar regulatory bodies in other countries. In the US, however, one court case has set the precedent under which NFTs act as securities and therefore should have to follow the rules established for these financial instruments.

The US Supreme Court, in the *SEC v W.J. Howey* (*Howey*) laid down four elements to determine whether digital assets such as cryptocurrencies or NFTs could be considered a "security" or "investment contract":

1. An investment of money…
2. into a common enterprise…
3. in which investors expect to profit…
4. from the efforts of third parties.

Any NFT that fulfills these four conditions is likely to be deemed to be a security by the SEC. The primary responsibility of regulating NFTs lies with the SEC and Commodity Futures Trading Commission (CFTC) under federal securities law. In addition, each state has its own securities law, which may have different or additional requirements to those of the federal securities law.

Several moves by regulators and private citizens are poised to make a clearer delineation of when NFTs and other digital assets stray into securities land:

- **Lawsuit over NBA Top Shot Moments**
  A Virginia resident filed a class-action lawsuit on behalf of anyone who has purchased NBA Top Shot Moments. The case accuses NFT creator Dapper Labs and the NBA of marketing and selling "unregistered securities." The plaintiff has alleged that NBA Top Shot Moments (digital video basketball cards) pass the Howey test and should be subject to the Securities Act of 1933. Dapper Labs responded with a motion before a Manhattan court requesting that the court dismiss the lawsuit as its digital basketball cards are simply collectibles like any other sports trading cards, coins, or stamps. The case is pending, and the final decision is likely to shed light on a number of issues related to the legal status of NFTs as securities.

- **SEC Scrutiny over Illegal NFT Offerings**
  Around the middle of the year, the SEC started scrutinizing NFT creators and crypto exchanges for securities violations. The scrutiny has been specifically geared toward ascertaining whether certain NFTs are being utilized to raise money like traditional securities. The SEC is particularly interested in fractional ownership of NFTs, which it believes looks a lot like owning shares in a company or project. Selling small pieces of more valuable NFTs is a big part of New Jersey-based crypto lending company BlockFi's business model. The SEC has ordered BlockFi to pay a record fine of $100 million for failing to list its "high yield" lending products as securities. More action could be forthcoming in light of SEC Chairman Gary Gensler characterization of "the vast majority" of the nearly 10,000 tokens in the crypto market as securities.

- **Litigation against Former Open Sea Executive**
  Former Open Sea executive Nate Chastain has been charged with insider trading - a phrase and an offense reserved for people accused of using proprietary information to buy or sell company stocks or other securities. It can be argued that the attempt by the Department of Justice (DOJ) to charge Chastain with insider training is actually an attempt to label at least some of the NFTs on the Open Sea marketplace as securities. OpenSea has instructed its employees to avoid using securities-related words such as "trading" and "derivative" when talking about the platform's NFTs.

- **Yuga Labs Threatened with Class Action Lawsuit**
  Bored Ape Yacht Club (BAYC) creator Yuga Labs was threatened with a class action lawsuit for "inappropriately inducing" investors to buy BAYC NFTs and ApeCoin. A law firm has alleged that Yuga Labs used celebrity promoters and endorsements to inflate the price of its NFTs by overpromising returns. They further alleged that this was in contravention of the US securities law.

- **Regulatory Action Sand Vegas Casino Club**
  In April 2022, securities regulators in Texas and Alabama issued a cease and desist order against Sand Vegas Casino Club, a Cyprus-based virtual casino developer, to stop selling NFTs on the grounds that they are unregistered securities. The states found that the company failed to take several important steps such as registering a physical address, warning against the risks of operating a casino, and registering the NFTs with the states in marketing the NFT to consumers and prospective investors in its metaverse and online gambling site.

- **Proposed Crypto Bill**
  In June 2022, US senators introduced a bipartisan bill calling for new rules on cryptocurrency and bestowing the bulk of

the responsibilities for regulating NFTs on the CFTC. If the bill passes, the CFTC and not the SEC will be responsible for regulating crypto products since the authors believe the currencies are more likely to operate as commodities than as securities. While the proposed bill does not explicitly mention NFTs, it is likely to be applied to them. This bill is expected to be discussed in the senate sometime early next year.

These legal developments suggest an increasing push in the US to categorize certain NFTs as securities. The legal categorization of NFTs as securities will have a huge impact on the video game industry and on emerging technologies companies aiming to launch their own NFTs as it would require potentially onerous compliance with US securities law. Non-compliance can attract heavy penalties; it is best to consult an NFT lawyer about the legal status of NFTs before embarking on an NFT project. A consultation can prevent legal liability down the road.

Several of the cases mentioned in this article are the subject of their own essays in this book. Please refer to those stories for updates. Meanwhile, the class-action suit against Dapper labs winds its way through the court system. Dapper filed a motion to dismiss in late August 2022, with the plaintiff's response due at the end of October and Dapper's reply to that response coming a month later.

NFT Litigation Offers Lessons For Emerging Tech Firms

The increased popularity of non-fungible tokens (NFTs) brings the potential to inspire new methods of creating and disseminating art within the digital landscape. The last year has witnessed a frenzy in the NFT space, including a wave of litigation commencing from the lawsuit against Dapper Lab and its CEO Roham Gharegozlou for alleged securities fraud to the most recent suit filed by Nike against StockX for trademark infringement. Understanding the legal issues and the financial ramifications involved in the litigation can

provide critical lessons for anyone interested in the NFT space.

Notable Cases

In February 2022, Nike alleged that the reseller had sold nearly 500 Nike brand sneaker NFTs, causing significant damage to the athleticwear company's reputation and legitimacy. The allegation followed French luxury group Hermès' legal proceedings against artist Mason Rothschild over the sale of Birkin Bag NFTs. Both these cases are pending and raise interesting questions related to trademark infringement, false designation of origin, trademark dilution, cybersquatting, and injury to business reputation. Once the final verdict on both these cases is out, legal precedents will likely emerge at the intersection of NFTs, creative liberties, intellectual property, and First Amendment rights.

The year 2021 also saw several high-profile cases related to NFTs which are likely to settle important aspects related to blockchain. For example, the first NFT-related litigation came with the Dapper Labs lawsuit. In May 2021, Virginia resident Jeeun Friel filed as the lead plaintiff in a class-action lawsuit against Dapper, perhaps best known as the developer of CryproKitties, and its CEO. Friel alleged in the New York State Supreme Court that the defendants violated the Securities Act of 1933 by actively promoting, offering, and selling NBA Top Shot Moments NFTs. She argues that Top Shot NFTs are digital assets that derive their value from the success or failure of a specific project, promoter, or start-up. That would categorize them as securities and as such, they should have been registered with the Securities and Exchange Commission (SEC). The court will decide whether NFTs are collectible securities.

Immediately, after Friel filed her case, in June 2021, Roc-A-Fella Records initiated a lawsuit against its co-founder Damon Dash for allegedly attempting to "mint" and sell Jay-Z's album *Reasonable Doubt* as an NFT. Roc-A-Fella's primary contention was that Dash did not own the rights to the album and therefore was prohibited from selling an NFT of the record via an auction. A federal district court in New York City ruled in favor of Roc-A-Fella and granted the label a temporary restraining order barring Dash from altering, selling, or otherwise disposing of any copyright or other property interest in *Reasonable Doubt*, including the auction of an NFT reflecting such interest.

Finally, in November 2021, production company Miramax sued *Pulp Fiction* director Quentin Tarantino in a California federal court, alleging breach of contract and copyright infringement. Miramax has argued that NFTs do not fall under Tarantino's limited contract rights for the film. It has specifically argued that even though Tarantino has the right to publish pieces of the script (film), NFTs do not fall under that publishing umbrella. This case also remains under judicial review. Once there is a final verdict on all these cases, we may gain a greater understanding of how NFTs will be classified and what rights remain with creators of the underlying asset, and what activities non-copyright-holders will be allowed to undertake.

Lessons For Emerging Technologies Companies

Whatever the courts decide, video game, extended reality, digital media, crypto, and other emerging technology companies can profit from understanding the decisions and establishing procedures to protect their own rights and avoid infringing on those of others:

1. **Pay Attention to Contracts**
   The Miramax/Tarantino/*Pulp Fiction* case especially cautions companies in the NFT space is the importance of careful negotiation and drafting of contracts. Parties should bargain to ensure that either they retain as many rights as possible or ensure they receive appropriate compensation for giving them up. Rights allocations should consider all future uses, including new and future technologies like NFTs. The Miramax lawsuit shows that the distributor's legal counsel and the contract drafters did not take into account the impact NFTs and blockchain would exert on the digital media industry. Nonetheless, Miramax's lawyers had the foresight to secure its client broad catch-all rights relating to their acquired IP surrounding the film. They used forward-thinking contractual language to describe the IP rights acquired.

2. **Ensure you have the requisite rights**
   Emerging technologies companies and video game developers should ensure that they have the right to mint, use, and market NFT-related content. Failure to do so could implicate them for infringing on copyrights and trademarks held by third parties. It is advised that all companies intending to use and monetize NFTs should carefully check whether they have the rights to leverage the underlying asset through an NFT offering. Sometimes, entities or stakeholders may only be granted residual ownership rights to the underlying asset, which may or may not allow them to create and profit from NFTs based on that asset.

3. **Conduct due diligence before purchasing NFTs** Interested NFT buyers, collectors, and investors should perform due diligence that the minter or other seller does indeed hold the IP rights needed to develop and market NFTs relating to the underlying asset. Inexperienced buyers should act as though the offer is fraudulent until they are convinced otherwise, as there are more shady NFTs deals than there are lucrative ones. Seek the counsel of an attorney to ensure that the NFT offering you are planning to participate in is legitimate. A lawyer experienced in NFTs and blockchain can also advise on the legality of the overall NFT offering, the legitimacy of what is being offered, and the scope of rights that would be acquired via the NFTs.

Conclusion

The recent spate of litigation in the NFT space presents a double-edged sword. The surge in cases is good news because it should provide guidance on crucial issues. Further, it paves the path for legal precedent to be set concerning crucial aspects such as intellectual property, Know Your Customer regulations, securities regulations, etc. Nonetheless, the rush to the courtroom could be a bad omen, rattling regulators' cages and spurring them to add regulatory burdens on companies and stakeholders in the NFT space. Given the surge in judicial cases related to NFTs, emerging technologies companies need to consult an attorney or a law firm specializing in the industry. Companies, rights holders, and other stakeholders in the NFT arena take their rights very seriously.

A month after the publication of this article, Husain's estate dropped its claim that the agreement to sell the Lightning *mural was partially negotiated in India. That would subject the transaction to Indian copyright law, under which Husain never conveyed the copyrights related to the modes or media Tamarind needs to use in order to complete its planned NFT project. With the counterclaim resolved, Tamarind's underlying lawsuit seeking a declaration that it does indeed own the rights necessary for the NFT project to move forward will now proceed without the counterclaims. Also, since publication, a Manhattan jury ruled in favor of Hermes, ordering Rothchild to pay restitution of $110,000 for trademark infringement and brand dilution and $23,000 for cybersquatting..*

Chapter and Metaverse: IP Cases in the Digital Space

Despite the current prevalence of NFTs, it is often unclear what legal rights they convey to the new owner upon resale. Owners of copyright and trademark assets underlying NFTs may claim legitimate rights that conflict with those that NFT

owners believe they possess. Below we examine legal questions related to NFTs and intellectual property (IP) rights, exclusivity, and other issues in light of recent lawsuits. We will also examine the impact of unsettled legal questions on the development of the metaverse and other next-generation technologies.

Copyright Holders' Rights To Mint NFTs of Their Works

Recently, New York-based art gallery Tamarind LLC received a cease and desist letter after announcing its plan to issue a series of NFTs based on a 60-foot-long mural known as *Lightning* or *The Guernica of India.* Artist Maqbool Fida Husain's estate claims in the letter that it maintains the copyright to the mural, which Tamarind purchased from the late artist for $400,000 in 2002. Tamarind disagrees, contending the purchase gives it the exclusive, worldwide, royalty-free license "to display, market, reproduce and resell all or any part of the artwork, including on all digital and off-line media."

Seeking relief from the cease and desist letter, Tamarind filed a complaint with the New York Federal Court on 21 January 2022 for a declaratory judgment stating that it can proceed to mint NFTs based on Husain's mural. The suit asserts that Husain agreed that he would no longer be the owner of the artwork or the intellectual property associated with it.

Rights of Trademark Holders To Mint NFTs

While the Tamarind/*Lightning* case hinges on whether the IP creator conveyed copyright and trademark rights to the buyer, other cases involve buyers minting NFTs based on IP for which they definitely have ***not*** received the trademark holder's blessing. For example, US-based sportswear giant Nike has sued StockX, an online resale marketplace selling NFTs of shoes, streetwear, and other goods, for trademark infringement, trademark dilution, and other violations.

Similarly, Hermès filed a lawsuit against Mason Rothschild for NFTs infringing the Birkin trademark. Such unauthorized use raises important questions regarding the NFT rights of trademark holders. As the NFT marketplace continues to expand, trademark holders are increasingly taking steps to protect their IP and assert exclusive rights to commercialize NFTs that depict or are otherwise based on their marks.

The Benelux Convention for Intellectual Property grants trademark holders the right to prohibit third parties from using identical or similar signs for similar or identical goods and/or services. For stakeholders in digital industries and verticals, that means that trademark infringement likely occurs if a third party uses the trademark without consent and registers the trademark for classifications linked to the metaverse, extended reality, video games, digital music, and art, collectibles, or NFTs. However, because NFTs are a fairly recent development and new use cases emerge daily, few companies have registered their trademarks for classes associated with the digital environment. Currently, no case law has been decided, adding to the confusion. To ensure their IP is fully protected, trademark owners should file trademark applications that encompass goods and services associated with the metaverse, virtual spaces, digital art, and NFTs.

Non-IP Claims

One recent high-profile case raises questions concerning the chain of title over NFTs. In *Free Holdings v McCoy*, the plaintiff, a Canadian entity, alleges that it owns artist Kevin McCoy's *Quantum*, which is regarded by many to be the first-ever NFT. Free Holdings brought a suit before New York's Southern District Court, claiming that auction house Sotheby's wrongly attributed ownership of the NFT when it sold the work for $1.47 million. Free Holdings asserts that it assumed the rights to the NFT after McCoy failed to renew his ownership. According to the suit, the blockchain on which McCoy minted *Quantum* requires that owners renew their rights every 250 days; McCoy let his ownership expire, and the NFT went unclaimed for years, Free Holdings says.

This case is important as it is the first to address the issue of what it truly means to own something minted using blockchain technology. While blockchain is supposed to provide a permanent and indisputable ledger of provenance, the complexity of the technology muddies the waters. The confusion is worsened by the inconsistent terms related to the transfer of content and ownership from one blockchain to another. The court's decision should create a long-sought precedent and help establish how courts view ownership as it relates to blockchain. It could also shed light on whether blockchain is in fact the game-changing innovation that many of its supporters claim it is.

Conclusion

These cases are likely to have profound implications on blockchain technology and its utility in proving digital ownership in the metaverse. It is hoped that they will answer questions including whether minting an NFT is the exclusive right of copyright owners, when and how NFTs violate trademark holders' rights, and whether minting NFTs is contrary to traditional legal principles protecting intellectual property. Of course, some of these cases may settle without providing any legal guidance or be resolved by holdings that cannot be used as general references for future cases. Regardless of the outcome, companies in the blockchain, metaverse, and digital asset space should periodically consult with an attorney or a law firm specializing in NFTs and other emerging technologies for up-to-date legal advice on the complexities and technicalities surrounding the rights of IP holders in these spaces.

This ruling gives NFT owners the same recourse as other rightful owners whose property is stolen. The judge made the ruling after considering that know your customer (KYC) regulations compelled OpenSea/Ozone to (and the platform apparently did) collect information that would enable investigators to track down the stolen NFTs and lead them to the identities of the thieves. The ruling is expected to give NFT and other crypto asset owners greater leverage in unmasking other types of blockchain fraud, as well. The ruling also clears up the question of jurisdiction. The High Court averred that because the alleged victim is a UK citizen, it has the authority to make such a ruling even though the defendant is located outside the UK.

UK Recognizes NFTs as Property: Implications for the US

Recently, the UK's High Court recognized non-fungible tokens (NFTs) as "property" separate from the underlying assets or objects they represent. This decision is likely to have far-reaching implications for disputes involving digital assets and digital art. The High Court's ruling is likely to influence

how the US views NFTs when it comes to trademark, copyright, and other intellectual property rights.

Background

In a landmark decision, the UK's High Court has ruled that NFTs are property, separate from the underlying content that they represent. The court rendered this decision in light of Lavinia Osbourne's stolen NFTs. Earlier in the year, Osbourne, founder of Women in Blockchain, claimed that two Boss Beauties NFTs were stolen from her Metamask wallet. Earlier in the year, Osbourne, founder of Women in Blockchain, claimed that two Boss Beauties NFTs were lifted from her Metamask wallet. Boss Beauties is an NFT collection linked to images of "beautifully diverse, empowered women." Osbourne did not provide details about how criminals were able to steal the NFTs, the tokens were later listed on OpenSea, the popular NFT marketplace. It seems that these NFTs ended up in the possession of two anonymous OpenSea account holders. Osbourne filed an injunction against OpenSea seeking to reclaim the NFTs. The court issued an injunction to freeze the assets on the accounts of Ozone Networks (the host of OpenSea) and compelled OpenSea to disclose information about the two account holders in possession of the stolen NFTs.

Legal Consequences

The outcome will bear on worldwide NFT, crypto, and blockchain law on several touchpoints.

First and most importantly, it removes the uncertainty—at least in the UK—about whether NFTs constitute property in and of themselves, distinct from the artwork, songs, tweets, or other "assets" they represent. The significance of this opinion is that the court held that an NFT represents a kind of asset that can be frozen, much like a bank or investment account. Nonetheless, this case also raises some ambiguity as the court remained silent on the relationship between an NFT and the underlying asset. As things stand, simple ownership of an NFT does not convey copyright, usage rights, moral rights, or any other rights. These rights must be explicitly granted in a written contract.

Second, the ruling clarifies that, contrary to the contention of many crypto supporters, code is not law. The term "code is law" is popular among crypto enthusiasts who believe in the proposition that written code is a legitimate form of legal enforcement even if the software contains a glitch or performs in an unintended manner. Practically speaking, it means that if someone obtains an NFT simply because they are able to access the rightful owner's private keys via phishing or other scams, it should not be considered illegal. The code, some would argue, enabled the activity, and the perpetrator acted in a manner that is consistent with and permitted by the code, whose jurisdiction should be respected. The High Court, however, took the view that a person's legitimate claim to a particular private key is legally significant. The fact that another party is capable of taking possession of an asset doesn't mean that ownership is conveyed or that they should be allowed to do so.

Third, the court issued an injunction against 'unknown persons' as the holders of the wallet containing the stolen NFTs remained incognito at the time the injunction was issued. Further, the court compelled OpenSea to provide information about the two account holders, shredding the cloak of anonymity many blockchain users find desirable when conducting financial transactions.

Finally, the court ordered OpenSea to freeze the relevant accounts so that the NFT could not be moved or traded. Rightful owners of NFTs will find such action a valuable method for preserving their intellectual property rights.

Freezing an asset and preventing it from being sold or moved to untraceable accounts will preserve the chain of evidence and give investigators time to unravel the events that led to the NFT's misappropriation. Following an investigation, legal action can then be initiated.

Implications for US Policy

The High Court's decision reinforces and coincides with the Internal Revenue Service's (IRS's) existing policy of viewing NFTs as property. The IRS and scholars share the view that NFTs possess all the traditional attributes of property. The owner can sell it, trade it, give it away, and prevent others from engaging with it. There is, however, some difference of opinion as to how completely separate jurisdictions can assure the security of an NFT. According to one view, the UK's official recognition of NFTs as property means that holders can be assured that their tokens will be secure and they will have legal recourse in the UK if their property were stolen. Conversely, other commentators have noted that since the US has not officially declared NFTs are property, NFT holders have no recourse if someone hacks into their wallet and steals an NFT. This has led some experts to opine that the UK is leading the way in preserving NFT ownership rights. The fact that NFTs already enjoy the status of property in the US, according to the IRS and other executive-branch agencies does little to fill the current legislative vacuum in assigning property rights to NFT holders. There is an urgent need for a federal law on digital assets, and discussions are underway.

Conclusion

This High Court's decision has helped clarify the important point that an NFT should be considered property and therefore is eligible to receive all the remedies and benefits of physical possessions. It is, however, unclear as to whether US courts will follow similar reasoning even though NFTs are already considered property in certain contexts in the US as well. This ambiguity has important consequences in determining the scope of protection extended by the NFT platforms. It is particularly unclear whether courts in the US will step up to protect stolen NFTs in the same way as the UK High Court. It is best to consult an attorney specializing in NFTs for advice about the best legal strategy to keep your NFTs secure. An attorney can also draft appropriate legal documents for protecting your digital assets.

World-class athletes, musical icons, and movie idols seem unable to resist the additional fame and bank account boost that come with lending their influence, image, and name to NFT projects. It may make sense for NFT creators to hitch their wagons to these stars to generate the buzz that can often propel a collection's value into six or seven figures. But doing so without the celebrity's express permission can land a minter in hot water. Where do fair use and free speech end and the right of publicity begin when it comes to NFTs?

Star Power: NFTs and the Right of Publicity

Lately, there has been a lot of buzz around celebrities endorsing or investing in NFTs. The trend raises several legal implications surrounding the minting of NFTs and the right of publicity. This article specifically delves into personality rights and outlines some strategies NFT minters should keep in mind while minting NFTs that are based on a celebrities' likenesses, images, name, or personality.

Background

It is important to understand the legal definition and nuances involved in publicity rights. The right of publicity (also known as 'personality rights') refers to an individual's right to control the commercial use of their name, image, likeness (NIL), and other aspects of their identity. In essence, it allows a person to keep his or her image and likeness from being commercially exploited without permission or compensation. The right of publicity varies by jurisdiction. About half of US states recognize a distinct right of publicity, stipulating the scope of an individual's right of publicity, the assignability of those rights, and the statutory damages for violating the right of publicity. Others view it as part of other protections such as the common-law right to privacy or statutes prohibiting unfair competition.

California has enacted the most comprehensive laws with regard to publicity. In the Golden State, a celebrity or well-known personality needs to prove four elements in order to prevail in a claim of violation of their right of publicity:

1. The defendant used the plaintiff's identity.

2. The defendant appropriated the plaintiff's name or likeness to the defendant's commercial or other benefits.

3. The appropriation was perpetrated without the plaintiff's consent.

4. The appropriation resulted in an injury to the plaintiff.

The above test essentially aims to protect individuals' proprietary interest in their own identity. The protected elements of a person's identity include name, likeness, voice, signature, and other uniquely identifying traits.

Licensing

If NFT minters fail to obtain express permission to use an individual's NIL, they may receive a cease and desist order demanding they discontinue all use of the individual's persona. Some letters may demand monetary compensation or threaten legal action. There is a very real possibility that an NFT minter who depicts a celebrity in an NFT without permission could be sued without the opportunity to negotiate a settlement. Being found in violation of a person's right of publicity can result in substantial monetary penalties. Further, depending on the state, the NFT platform/marketplace may be held contributorily liable for allowing the sale of the infringing NFT. If the NFT minter used the platform to create, mint, or sell the offending NFT, the creator may be obligated to indemnify the site per its terms of use.

Free Speech

One of the fundamental questions that arises when assessing the right of publicity is whether celebrity endorsement of NFTs constitutes free speech. Over the years, hundreds of cases have contemplated how the right of publicity claims relate to the First Amendment. A key issue in many of these cases is whether the claimed violation was intended for commercial use; the right to control one's persona is not intended to supersede the five freedom protections deemed necessary to ensure an independent press and open expression in art and entertainment.

In California, where many rights of publicity cases are litigated, the relevant statute protects only against the unauthorized uses of one's NIL "in products, merchandise, or goods…for purposes of advertising or selling." Determining whether a work is "commercial," however, is made more difficult due to a lack of judicial clarity. In fact, it has not been definitively determined whether depicting an individual in a non-commercial NFT without that person's consent constitutes a violation of that person's right of publicity or whether it should be considered protected speech. Until the courts deliver a definitive ruling, publicity rights claims against NFTs will continue to be decided on a case-by-case basis.

Best Practices to Avoid Right of Publicity Claims

Projects and businesses that plan to or currently use NFTs for commercial purposes should protect themselves by implementing strict policies before minting NFTs based on a celebrity or on an individual's NIL:

- ***Seek permission or licensure***
  For minters intent on depicting a real person (alive or dead, celebrity or average Joe) in an NFT, the safest course of action is to license that person's persona for use in the NFT. Licensing content is common practice, but the process takes time and money. It is also a good idea to license the rights over specific images, as the majority of the NFTs are based on existing images. To minimize potentially damaging legal risk, it is best to engage an attorney to draft the license agreement.

- ***Create a disclaimer***
  Having appropriate disclaimers in place can minimize the risk of NIL claims. Such a disclaimer should stipulate the background information, intended usage, and the terms of the license. Consult an attorney or a law firm specializing in intellectual property and NFTs to help you in drafting a disclaimer.

- ***Rely on publicly available resources***
  It is advisable to base NFTs on publicly available records such as property records and public financial information as minting an NFT based on such

information runs a reduced risk of being deemed an invasion of someone's privacy. In these cases, copyright ownership and related requirements should be closely observed.

As the popularity of NFTs continues to soar, projects and businesses intending to mint their own NFTs should be aware of the legal risks associated with using an individual's likeness without their consent. Even though you might have the necessary licenses and permissions, you might not be completely insulated from legal liability since certain forms of statutory legal protections may still leave grounds for claims. Consequently, legal advice from a qualified legal professional is highly advisable at every stage of bringing an NFT to market.

While the applicability of this ruling in the US and other western countries may be limited. It is interesting to consider the Chinese tribunal's assertion that marketplace platforms accept fiduciary responsibilities if they collect a commission or otherwise benefit financially from transactions conducted there. That duty includes taking reasonable measures to verify the legal ownership of the intellectual property attached to an NFT. In recognizing the NFT owner's exclusive right to sell it, the court not only ordered the platform to pay damages but also to confiscate the counterfeit material and confine it to an inaccessible virtual lockbox (Once created, NFTs cannot be permanently deleted).

Not-So-Bored Aping:
Chinese Copyright Law and the US Courts

A Chinese court's ruling on copyright infringement of NFTs could define how tokens and other digital assets are viewed by regulators in the United States and around the world. The court found that an NFT platform is liable for contributory copyright infringement with respect to a digital artwork it

hosted. In addition, the ruling touched upon other related issues such as intermediary liability and the applicability of safe harbor provisions to NFT platforms. Here, we will examine the decision, review how US courts have ruled in similar cases, and analyze how the Chinese decision may influence future cases in the US.

Background

Hangzhou Internet Court decided that NFT hosting and commercial platforms are responsible for the digital works traded there. The plaintiff, Shenzhen Qice Diechu Cultural Creativity Co., alleged that Hangzhou Yuanyuzhou Technology Co., Ltd. infringed upon its copyright to a series of "Fat Tiger" illustrations. The defendant operates an NFT marketplace and digital art trading platform called Bigverse. The plaintiff initiated the lawsuit after finding that a third party had created a digital illustration identical to its copyrighted work (down to the artist's Weibo watermark) and sold an NFT that uses the image on Bigverse.

The plaintiff claimed that, as a specialized NFT marketplace, Bigverse assumes a heightened obligation to monitor artwork hosted on its platform. According to the plaintiff, Bigverse must protect copyright holders' intellectual property by conducting preliminary reviews to determine whether users who create and market NFTs on the site actually hold the copyrights to the underlying artworks. Failure to do so, the plaintiff argued, constitutes contributory infringement.

The defendant sought refuge in the safe harbor rule, which intends to shield ISPs that provide passive distribution and facilitation services for copyrighted works. Bigverse argued that, as an intermediary, it should not be liable for damages incurred as a result of the sale of counterfeit artwork and that its obligation only extends as far as taking down works upon receiving a notice of infringement from a copyright holder.

The Hangzhou Internet Court ruled in favor of the plaintiff, effectively narrowing the interpretation of safe harbor. The court held that Bigverse was liable for copyright infringement as a transaction involving an NFT digital work is subject to the copyright holder's right of information network dissemination under the People's Republic of China's copyright law. The court decided the nature of the plaintiff's business in actively promoting not only the distribution but also the creation of copyrighted works carries an additional burden of care in deterring intellectual property infringement. It should have taken the proactive step to prevent the NFT from being uploaded rather than reactively taking it down when its authenticity came into question.

In ruling for the plaintive, the court ordered compensatory damages of $600 to cover the economic loss and reasonable legal expenses incurred.

Applicability to the US

The fundamental question arising from this case is whether the US courts will agree with the Chinese decision that the intermediary liability exception contained within safe harbor standards does not apply to NFT platforms. Our view is that domestic judges would reaffirm safe harbor for these platforms and not hold them contributorily liable in the event of copyright infringement. This is due to the policy and legal considerations explained below:

US Policy: Chinese Judicial Trends

There has been a strong recent trend among Chinese courts to strip e-commerce platforms of their liability protections. Responding to strong government criticisms and retaliatory actions against e-commerce companies in China, courts have taken an activist stance, not just regarding copyright but also on other issues such as real-name authentication and data protection. There is no policy reason for an open society and free-enterprise system such as exists in the US to over-regulate these sites or hold them responsible for the third-party content they host.

US Jurisprudence: Safe Harbor Precedent

Internet providers, social media sites, and other online communications networks have enjoyed the safe harbor provisions outlined in the Digital Millennium Copyright Act (DMCA) for nearly 25 years. US courts likely would not exclude NFT platforms from this precedent. In fact, some NFT marketplaces claim safe harbor protections within their terms of service. There are certain situations, however, in which the courts may consider that a platform's participation in NFT creation and sales nullifies safe harbor. For instance, an NFT marketplace may lose protection if it receives any financial benefit directly attributable to the infringing activity, takes any action in selecting the content it hosts or modifies the content after it is uploaded and before it is transmitted to the audience. As such, the system of receiving fees for sales, either from the buyers or the sellers, could cost the platforms their ability to rely on the DMCA safe harbors. This also suggests that the American courts may hold differently if a similar case comes before it.

US Legislation: The Future of NFTs

In recent times, Congress has shown some willingness to address the shortcomings of the existing DMCA procedures. In 2020, Senator Thom Tillis released a discussion draft of his Digital Copyright Act, which is likely to significantly reform the DMCA. It is expected that in 2022 Congress may return to the question of updating the DMCA takedown regime. Consequently, it is likely that any decision on the liability of NFT platforms by US courts would be codified in future iterations.

Conclusion

The Chinese court ruling established a landmark regarding the rights and liabilities of NFT platforms. Only time will tell how the courts in the US will rule when a similar case comes before them. Given the weight of authorities and current precedents in the US, it seems that NFT e-commerce sites may find recourse in the safe harbor rule and avoid liability for contributing to copyright infringement simply by hosting dubious art or digital works, provided they do not profit directly from their sale. Nonetheless, due to impending changes to the DMCA take-down provisions and the complexity of the issues involved, it is recommended that NFT platforms and related parties should seek up-to-date advice from an attorney or a law firm specializing in NFTs if any potential risk is identified. In particular, having well-drafted legal documents, especially with regard to DMCA take-downs, is extremely important for mitigating legal liability under the DMCA.

Just weeks after suing StockX over its NFT offering, Nike upped the stakes by claiming the sneaker resale site knowingly allowed counterfeit Nike footwear to be sold on the site. StockX questions both the timing of the amended lawsuit and the latest claims' veracity. StockX contends that its sneaker-validation process has "revolutionized the industry by creating a process in which 100% of products on its platform are authenticated by trained human..." The NFT portion of the dispute likely will hinge on whether the court buys StockX's claim that the NFTs it mints depicting Nike sneakers hold no intrinsic value because they are not digital assets or "virtual products." They merely give owners access to and represent ownership of the shoes they own and store with StockX.

Nike Kicks Up a Fuss Over StockX Sneaker NFTs

StockX is a leading online sneaker and streetwear marketplace that, like dozens of other retailers, recently plunged into the NFT pool. Earlier this year, StockX announced its VaultNFT collection of digital avatars of real-

world sneakers. Not long afterward, Nike also ventured into the NFT universe when it mobilized RTFKT Studios, which it had acquired in late 2021. Nike filed a lawsuit against StockX for a host of intellectual property (IP) infringement claims. Welcome to the Metaverse, where blockchain and IP law collide in a cosmos of lawlessness.

As the case plays out, we look at the legal issues involved.

Background to the NFT Feud

StockX serves as an online marketplace where consumers can buy and sell high-end shoes and streetwear. It was founded in 2015 by Quicken Loans founder and CEO Dan Gilbert. He then purchased Campless from Josh Luber—an online repository for sneaker sales data that was the predecessor of StockX. Operating much like eBay, it has become one of the most popular online destinations for consumers to purchase hard-to-find luxury shoes and streetwear.

On January 18, 2022, StockX diversified into the NFT marketplace with the launch of its VaultNFTs collection. However, rather than selling NFTs based purely upon art such as photographs, drawings, paintings, and the like, the online resale platform has created an NFT-based avatar system for physical sneakers held in its inventory. The sneakers are minted "under custodial authority" as ERC-1155 tokens on the Ethereum blockchain. While the e-commerce platform sells myriad brands, the VaultNFT avatars are a proverbial step forward as they tie the NFTs to physical items, primarily Nike-branded shoes.

Nike's purchase of RTFKT Studios—an NFT sneaker brand where one sale earned it $3.1 million in seven minutes—launched the sportswear giant onto another plane of existence. The move was true to form; Nike has always been about style and substance, using forward-thinking engineering and innovative materials to always stay one step ahead of its competitors. In February, Nike filed suit against StockX in the New York Southern District Court, alleging that StockX committed trademark infringement, trademark dilution, and related causes of action with its virtual products registered on the blockchain.

The First Sale Doctrine and Lawsuit Details

The overarching issue in this case is whether or how the "first sale doctrine" applies to digital goods. The first sale doctrine is a legal principle that states a copyright or trademark owner cannot prevent a consumer who has lawfully purchased a copyrighted good—such as a CD—from selling, lending, or giving that item to another person. This principle permits the distribution (or resale) of the copyrighted materials after the initial sale by the copyright owner. Without the first sale doctrine, no person, business, or non-profit entity would be able to resell their Nikes, lend a novel, or auction a Norman Rockwell. Federal copyright law has codified the first sale doctrine, stating "the owner of a particular copy or phonorecord lawfully made under this title, or any person authorized by such owner, is entitled, without the authority of the copyright owner, to sell or otherwise dispose of the possession of that copy or phonorecord." With trademarks, the resale of an item bearing a trademark is permissible unless it is likely to confuse or deceive consumers—courts have recognized these limitations for trademarks and the first sale doctrine.

The first sale doctrine predates the digital era but is still applicable. While NFTs are digital assets, copyrights and trademarks still apply, especially if the NFT represents an image, slogan, song or a sports clip. For copyright purposes, does the first sale doctrine apply to NFTs minted in the image of Nike shoes, which are linked to the actual physical asset available for purchase? Does the trademark exception apply because consumers may be confused or deceived about the relationship between StockX and Nike? How should these rights be balanced? The issues are further complicated because there are no standard terms applicable to the grant of rights in the art underlying NFTs. Until general rules are promulgated, these issues will be resolved on a piecemeal basis.

To date, the *Nike v. StockX* case has generated more questions than answers regarding ownership, creative freedom, public domain, and fair usage in the NFT marketplace and digital assets in general. In its complaint, Nike raises five causes of action: 1) Trademark Infringement; False Designation of Origin / Unfair Competition; 3) Trademark Dilution; 4) Injury To Business Reputation and Dilution; 5) Common Law Trademark Infringement and Unfair Competition; it seeks a jury trial and monetary damages. Nike has several federally registered trademarks for its shoes that it claims StockX is "using Nike's trademarks to market, promote, and attract potential purchasers to its Vault NFTs" because there is no collaboration between Nike and StockX, which the latter is

Nike asserts that "StockX has chosen to compete in the NFT market not by taking the time to develop its own intellectual property rights, but rather by blatantly freeriding, almost exclusively, on the back of Nike's famous trademarks and associated goodwill." Further, Nike claims that the VaultNFTs based upon Nike footwear are an "unauthorized and infringing use of Nike's famous marks." Nike's lawyers also contend that StockX "minted" a Nike-branded NFT as an "investable digital asset" that it sold at a "heavily inflated" market price to "unsuspecting consumers" who are buying these tokens likely thinking they are approved by Nike.

Nike argues that it owns the copyrights and intellectual property rights to its real-world sneakers and that VaultNFTs avatars infringe upon these rights. VaultNFT owners can "redeem" the avatars as coupons for lowering the cost of obtaining real Nike shoes unless StockX exercises its right to not redeem the shoes under the contract. Additionally, Nike possesses common law rights in asserted marks used in connection with its goods and services in interstate commerce for the sale, distribution, promotion, and advertising. The company asserts that these marks extend to virtual products and that Nike intends to expand that use with current trademark applications by transferring them into the virtual market with its own NFTs.

Ultimately, Nike argues that the first sale doctrine does not apply in this case, allowing it to retain its IP rights because they do not transfer with the sale of its shoes. Once the shoes are sold from their stores, Nike has no say as to how they are distributed or resold. However, Nike does have a say as to how its image is used and who can profit from it.

Meanwhile, StockX contends that each of its VaultNFTs is tied to a specific product sold on its marketplace—a product StockX bought second-hand from a rightful owner/consumer. StockX says its right to use Nike branding and imagery falls within the first sale doctrine, so no copyright issues are pertinent. Further, Nike's IP rights do not entitle Nike to control transactions in the shoes after the first sale. So, StockX can buy the shoes from a retailer or an individual and resell them as it wishes, while using Nike's branding and imagery of the shoes in a limited way as part of the resale and marketing process. StockX argues that its NFTs are tied to the resale of Nike shoes on its marketplace, and they are not original NFTs creating digital versions of Nike's shoes. Rather, the NFTs offer proof of ownership of these goods that is recorded on the blockchain.

Copyrights can be divisible by contract from an asset or good. This aspect can be recorded on the blockchain so it will be traceable. However, NFTs are considered indivisible assets, meaning they cannot be sliced into fractional shares like cryptocurrency. Perhaps NFTs will evolve similarly to software, where NFT creators will need to obtain licensing rights from IP holders to showcase a copyrighted product. NFT and blockchain-related law is still evolving to deal with these new technologies. As the story unfolds, the *Nike v. StockX* case is likely to provide new legal insight as to how intellectual property rights will evolve to include NFTs and blockchain-related issues.

The parties in this high-profile case reached a settlement in June 2022. It was agreed that Damon Dash's status as a co-owner of the Rock-A-Fella record label does not give him the right to sell any portion of the company's corporate assets. Dash, therefore, is not allowed to sell an NFT of Jay-Z's Reasonable Doubt *album but is within his rights in selling his stake in the label. The settlement acknowledges that the album does indeed constitute a corporate asset, and all the rights to it belong to the label. Neither Dash, Jay-Z, nor any other shareholder "holds a direct ownership interest in* Reasonable Doubt.*"*

Jay-Z vs. Damon Dash: Lessons for Emerging Tech Firms

Rapper Jay-Z's legal beef with record executive Damon Dash entangles old-school creativity and newfangled technology, providing lessons for performers, promoters, developers, and anyone else involved in the art world. The disagreement between two-thirds of the founding brain trust behind Roc-A-Fella Records centers on the ownership and regulation of

non-fungible tokens (NFTs) and is likely to open a flurry of issues related to NFTs. This post examines the legal issues which are likely to come up before the courts in this case, and its potential impact on emerging technologies companies, especially video game developers.

Background

In 1996, Jay-Z teamed up with Damon Dash to sell CDs of his debut album *Reasonable Doubt*. In June 2021, Dash started an auction to sell this album as an NFT. Jay-Z's record label Roc-A-Fella sued Dash in order to stop him from auctioning off the copyright to the album as an NFT. Roc-A-Fella's contention was that the copyright in the album was held exclusively by Jay-Z and that Dash did not have the legal right to sell the album even though Dash held a one-third stake in the record label. Dash on the other hand argued that he never intended to sell his interest in *Reasonable Doubt* and that he never minted an NFT to reflect his ownership stake either in the album or in Roc-A-Fella.

U.S. District Court Judge John Cronan issued a temporary restraining order prohibiting Dash from selling the album as an NFT. Since Dash and his lawyers did not turn up for the hearing, the suit is likely to continue, and the court is likely to decide the surrounding legal issues related to NFTs. With the scene set, now we will delve into some of the potential legal issues which are likely to come up before the court and what they mean for emerging technologies companies.

Legal Issues

These are some of the legal issues that we expect to come up before the court in Jay Z's legal dispute with Damon Dash.

- ***Ownership***—Roc-A-Fella Records has argued that while Dash holds a one-third stake in the company, it is the company that owns the album itself, and he has no legal right to sell the NFT. The primary issue which is likely to come before the court is who holds the right to convert the album into an NFT. Can only the copyright owner mint NFTs from existing works or can the right to mint NFTs for existing works be assigned to a third party? Presently, there is no clear-cut answer to these issues. In any case, this case is a reminder of the complex issues involved in determining who can mint NFTs from existing works. It also brings to the fore the importance of copyright registration and the need for a solid license agreement before assigning or licensing copyright to a third party.

- ***Distribution***—Usually, an NFT can be created, or "minted" legally only with the consent of the owner of the underlying work. In order to mint an NFT, the software that generates the NFT must make a copy of the content file. Doing so without the consent of the intellectual property owner amounts to copyright infringement. The fundamental questions likely to come before the courts are, "If the NFT is made without the authorization of the copyright owner, does the *resale* of the NFT also constitute copyright infringement?" If such a sale is deemed to be akin to reselling a counterfeit book or a musical composition, there is no clarity on the legality surrounding the use and distribution of NFTs by third parties. This legal issue is significant for video game companies as they often provide players with digital collectibles and virtual in-game items. The issue extends beyond the Jay-Z Damon Dash beef. To ensure transparency, video game companies have started defining them as individual, 'non-replaceable' NFTs. Hence, video game companies, AR/VR firms; digital music producers, as well as record labels must ensure that they have the right to convert digital assets into NFTs.

- ***Right to Sell***—Another key question likely to come up before the courts is "Who has the right to sell the NFTs?" Roc-a-Fella Records is likely to argue that, since it holds the copyright to *Reasonable Doubt*, Jay-Z's debut album, it has the right to sell the NFT. The original auction on SuperFarm was canceled, but Roc-a-Fella Records was concerned that Damon Dash would attempt to sell the NFT again even though Judge Cronan issued a temporary restraining order. This case is a reminder about taking timely advice on copyright issues. It is in particular a reminder that professional legal assistance should be sought for drafting the agreement on the right to sell.

- ***Securities Regulation***—The court also will have to decide whether NFTs are securities and therefore subject to regulation by the US Securities and Exchange Commission (SEC). According to broker-dealer Arkonis Capital LLC, NFTs have tremendous potential value but do not function as traditional securities and do not fit clearly under the existing legal framework. The SEC is likely to take an interest, however, when NFT minters make their tokens look like or act as securities. This may prove the case when NFTs are obtained through fractional ownership (like shares of stock) or distribute revenues from subsequent sales. Hence, it is likely that the court may touch upon the financial categorization of NFTs' status and whether they can be considered securities under the Securities and Exchange Act of 1934.

- ***Copyright assignment and license***— Some commentators argue that the purchase of an NFT is simply a transfer of ownership from one person to another and that no copyright assignment or licensing takes place. Conversely, some contend that the purchase of NFTs is a form of copyright assignment. This view runs into trouble, as buying an NFT does not confer ownership of the underlying work to the purchaser unless explicitly provided by the owner of the underlying IP. However, since there is little case law on copyright infringement of digital art, there is no clarity surrounding copyright assignment and licenses related to NFTs. In any case, the purchase or sale of NFTs involves several gray areas, especially with respect to contract drafting and interpretation. Given the complexities of copyright licensing, legal advice from a sufficiently qualified lawyer should be sought before buying or selling NFT.

Conclusion

The Jay-Z Damon Dash legal encounter brings to light 99 Problems and opens a pandora's box of legal issues related to NFTs that until now have not been subjected to judicial review. Further litigation involving NFTs is expected as there are presently no clear rulings or directives on how to regulate NFTs. While the suit may ensure there Ain't No Love lost between Jay-Z and Dash, it also serves as a warning to buyers and sellers of NFTs to make sure both sides know exactly what's being sold. It also highlights the importance of expert legal advice at every stage leading to digital art being minted as an NFT.

GAMMA LAW®

media | technology | innovation

About Gamma Law

Gamma Law is a specialty Web3 law firm providing premium support to select clients in cutting-edge media/tech industry sectors. The firm provides clients the support required to succeed in complex business environments, push the boundaries of innovation, and achieve their objectives, both in the United States and internationally.

Website: https://gammalaw.com/
Email: info@gammalaw.com
Phone: +1 (415) 901-0510

Twitter: @GammaLaw
Facebook: https://www.facebook.com/GammaLaw
LinkedIn: https://www.linkedin.com/company/gamma-law/

Made in the USA
Columbia, SC
27 January 2024

31006416R00113